How to Be
Awkward

Essays

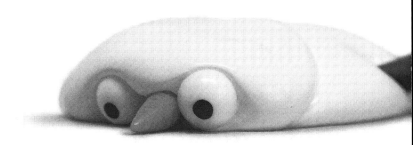

by Amanda Turner

FEVER STREAK PRESS

How to Be Awkward
Copyright © 2022 Amanda Turner
All rights reserved.

ISBN: 978-0-9986541-3-3

Design by Jeanne Core, DesignWorks Creative, Inc.

CONTENTS

INTRODUCTION

In my mind, I'm a goddamn cheetah. Sleek, stealthy, lithe, with a teaspoon of danger. I don't know, maybe more puma than cheetah, because pumas are a little more filled out, less lanky and scrawny. (No one has ever accused me of being lanky and scrawny.)

But still…

In my mind, I have seductive eyes, and that fleshy part that connects my neck to my chin isn't there.

I'm more graceful than lumbering, more ballerina than lumberjack.

I'm trustworthy and can hold my liquor and never finish a lunch date realizing that there's a crumbly bit peeking out from one nostril.

My voice is smooth and clear, like the mesmerizing fall of warm honey into chamomile tea. Nothing nasal about it.

I'm lavender scented like overpriced soap.

I'm not too much of this or that, but just the right amount. I'm the porridge that Goldilocks ate, but hopefully less lumpy than how I imagine porridge to be. Never mind. I don't want to be porridge.

But still…

There's the me in my mind. She's badass. She knows who she is and what she wants (*and then takes it!*).

She's quintessentially cool.

In reality, my body leaks and creaks and sweats. I have

overactive salivary glands. I'm serious; it's a thing. I know, because I have it. Go ahead; put that jealousy right back in your handbag.

I'm the woman in the bathroom stall next to you, hoping you'll hurry up and leave because I'm internally wrestling gastrointestinal issues and hoping you're not present for the inevitable, external conclusion of those issues.

I was the mullet-wearing child with thick, Coke-bottle bifocals. Now, I'm the forty-something who once again has braces on her teeth. Also, my right eye crusts over at night.

If you ever need to know where the antifungal nail treatment is in the grocery store, I'm your huckleberry.

I grow lone, thick hairs in odd places. Not on purpose.

I have a history of turning the most innocuous of circumstances into catastrophes of unimaginable awkwardness. I'm gifted that way.

My ability to land in cringeworthy situations and/or directly cause them is something I'm compelled to share and spread throughout the world, like goodwill and herpes. The stories that follow, these are my herpes.[1]

ö Ö ö

---

[1] *Please note, I do not have herpes.*

CHAPTER 1
I'M WHAT SMELLS BAD

You know the old sci-fi trope of a living brain in a jar? It had wires attached to it, allowing communication with its minions and foes. It was meant to be grotesque, but I see many benefits of such an existence. You'd always be comfortable, just floating there in formaldehyde like a giant pickle at the deli counter. You'd never have to contend with diarrhea or body shame. Someone else would have to deal with distasteful tasks, like when a cat gifts you with a headless bird on your doorstep. You could never be peer pressured into P90X or Zumba. Brains in jars don't agonize over those jiggly parts under the arms. They never experience a painful butt pimple. It seems like a fairly good setup to me.

Socially, a brain in a jar wouldn't have to suffer through small talk. The only idle chatter I might come up with to say to a brain in a jar would be, "My, you're looking very smart today." Beyond that, you'd get right down to business. Above all, a brain in a jar would never have to contend with awkward or embarrassing situations.

There's a sweet spot in childhood, somewhere after consciousness of what it is to be human—but before awareness of just how *awkward* it is to be human—when kids are like brains in jars. They just exist. No anxiety or shame. No fear of falling or failing.

The first inkling that my carefree state of being was

coming to an end was when a neighbor kid said that I should wear a shirt if I was going to play outside. I asked him why. He responded by pointing at my nipples, from one to the other and back again, as if they were clear markers of transgression.

"So?" I asked. He might as well have indicated my elbows or my feet.

Should I point his nipples out to him? I wondered. *Doesn't he realize he has them too?* And what on earth does that have to do with wearing a shirt? After all, it was the height of summer heat. Why would anyone wear a shirt?

Comfortable in my own skin, I didn't know any other way to be. I was equally comfortable in my KangaROOS, my worn-at-the-toes red shoes with silver Velcro straps. The ROOS had little pockets on the sides where I'd store my lunch money. They went best with my denim overalls, in which I felt I could conquer the world.

Those memories are enamoring, that feeling before the weight of being awkward and human settled on my shoulders and refused to leave. Before acne and anxiety; before the awareness of a society that not only has rules, but also the audacity to expect things of you. That feeling is fleeting, and once it's gone, it can't be restored. It's like popping a balloon or peeing one's pants, both of which I've done. Once it's out, you can't put it back in.

If only I'd recognized that freedom and known that it wouldn't last, I could have enjoyed it more. I might have savored it with my eyes closed as if feeling the sun on my face. In truth, I'm not a big fan of sun on my face. It brings my sweat mustache into full bloom, and I worry about cancer forming on the tip of my nose. Should a doctor ever need to remove the tip of my nose, I hope they'll be able to reconstruct it somehow, perhaps with cartilage from my ear. But then what would they use to reconstruct my ear? My other ear? Why not just use that ear in the first place? You can see the dilemma of rearranging one's facial cartilage. These are worries with which a brain in a jar does not have to contend.

When I was six, my time in that carefree existence came to an end on the day I was sure I had ruined my elementary school. I wasn't at the center of a cheating scandal or dealing crack on the playground. What I mean is that I ruined the actual school, the building itself, something I've never admitted until just now.

If you went to my elementary school and you remember the day it was ruined, when you emerged from your class at the chime of the last bell to find the air so putrid that it was hard to breathe, that was my fault. I find it's often the case that if you're looking for the source of something offensive, you're probably looking for me.

I'm the problem.

I'm what smells bad.

On the day I ruined the school, I had no need for lunch money tucked away in my ROOS. The night before, my mother had offered to pack my lunch.

"Would you like an egg salad sandwich?" she'd asked.

Boy, would I! An egg salad sandwich was a gourmet treat, a rare deviation from the usual peanut butter options: peanut butter and jelly, peanut butter and honey, or peanut butter and banana. Years later, I would feed peanut butter to a Labrador and realize what I must have looked like in the lunchroom.

But egg salad was something special. It took greater effort on my mother's part. This I knew. My mother did not take on many recipes that required more than a few steps. And for egg salad, eggs had to go through many stages—boiled and cooled and peeled and chopped—to yield that mayonnaise-heavy, delightfully soft delicacy that makes my mouth water to this day.

Note: perhaps we can dispense with use of the phrase "makes my mouth water." Because we all know we're not talking about water, right? It's saliva. Spit. The dentist who used to marvel at how much "water" my mouth produced wasn't fooling anyone; he was clearly identifying the fact that I have overactive salivary glands. At the time, I secretly believed that everyone might harbor a superpower. Some people might go through life never discovering what theirs was. What a shame that would be, not to realize that all along you were capable of flying or shooting lasers from your eyes or opening even the stubbornest of pickle jars, all because you never unlocked your superpower. I was devastated that the dentist might have just shed light on mine. That was my superpower, my destiny, my means of making the world a better place—I produce a lot of spit.

As she assembled my lunch, my mother, environmental advocate before her time, impressed upon me the importance of bringing my brown paper lunch bag home so that it might be reused. Maybe it was less about cutting down on waste and more about frugality. We qualified as poor at the time, and I knew that everything new required money, even brown paper bags.

What neither my mother nor I considered was that paper is porous and that eggs are smelly. At school, as I crossed the blacktop, peppered with its four square arenas and hopscotch courses, I gave no thought to the fact that packed lunches did not enjoy the luxury of refrigeration. And as mentioned before, ours was not the household to spring for Ziploc sandwich bags. We used the fold-over kind, which sometimes kept their contents in place, and sometimes not.

The sandwich was fine at lunchtime, the delicious respite from peanut butter that I'd been looking forward to, and I ate it completely and quickly. But by the end of the school day, though I'd long since consumed my sandwich, the odor of hard-boiled egg had somehow permeated the bag and then flooded into every crevice of the elementary school hallway, where our cubbies resided.

I didn't yet know this as the bell rang, children poured forth from their classrooms, and a collective groan filled the air in response to the stench.

"Oh my *GOD!*"

"What *is* that?"

And that which is the favorite question of many children, "Who farted?" No matter that no single person could have possibly passed that volume of gas.

Children sneered and snickered, plugging their noses or bringing their T-shirts up to cover their faces. Even the inside of a child's T-shirt after a hot day on the playground smelled better at that moment than the hallway of the school. A rowdy group of boys began showing off their skills (perhaps superpowers) by making farting noises with their armpits, because it seemed the right thing to do at the time.

Teachers lost all pretense of stoicism. Their heads popped briefly out of their classroom doors, like Whack-a-Mole, hovering just long enough to get a whiff of the hallway. For half a second their faces contorted with disgust—brows furrowing, noses scrunching, frowns forming—before they withdrew into their classrooms, locking their doors behind them.

Truth oozed over my brain like a pierced yolk when I

approached my cubby and realized that I was the epicenter of the stench. Perhaps some wayward egg salad shrapnel had been left behind and was the culprit, though I rarely left even the tiniest bit uneaten. Or maybe the eggs my mother used had been radioactive (and therefore extra smelly) and would bestow upon me a greater superpower than overactive salivary glands. One could hope.

It was definitely me. The odor filling the hallway like liquid, the stench that, were it visible, might resemble the deadly, gelatinous title character of the 1958 cinematic masterpiece *The Blob*, emanated from my cubby. And there was no Steve McQueen to save me. I was the problem.

I would imagine that cooler people have different memories of their first realizations. When you're a child and you're hit by that initial undeniable truth, it should be that you're loved or special or unique. Or, if you prefer something less self-centered, maybe a dawning of the great, vast world around you. But my first realization, which I remember as clearly as I can conjure that odor into my nose, was this: *I'm what smells bad.*

I hesitated before pulling the brown paper bag from my cubby, afraid that when I did so, the others would know that I was the source. If my suspicion of radioactive eggs proved true, I imagined the bag might have an otherworldly green glow to it, a sure tell that would alert all of my classmates to the fact that their olfactory discomfort was all my fault.

There was only one course of action: complete denial. I would take no ownership, and I would follow the herd. I immediately began echoing the grumblings of my classmates. "Yeah, gosh. What's that awful smell? That's really bad. Man-oh-man, someone sure farted a lot."

Hand in hand with denial came the next step—I would flee the scene of the crime. *This is what the bad guys do*, I thought. *Am I really a bad guy? Like one of the grotesquely masked villains on* Scooby-Doo? I'd never mentally cast myself in that role before. I wasn't so haughty as to compare myself with the beautiful Daphne, and freely admitted that Velma had a genius to which I could never aspire. Honestly, I most related to Shaggy, and secretly harbored a crush on Scrappy, if having a crush on an animated, obnoxious canine is even possible.[2]

I tugged uncomfortably at the straps of my overalls, grabbed my backpack and the offensive brown paper bag, and hightailed it out of that hallway as fast as my red and silver KangaROOS would allow, discreetly dropping the bag into the trash can outside the main doors. I can picture myself hustling out of the school. *Welcome to awkwardness*, I want to say to the younger me. *It's with you for life.*

I wondered what would happen to the school. I didn't understand that time and cleaning products would resolve the issue. I felt certain that I had permanently destroyed this educational institution. Adults often warned that if kids ruined something, they would have to pay for it. *If the principal found out it was me, would I have to pay for it? How much did a school cost? Were there security cameras that would be used in court? Would they find the bag and fingerprint it? Would I go to jail? And if so, would I be allowed to bring my nighttime companion, Pot-Belly Bear?*

When I told my mother of the debacle later that evening, she looked surprised and asked casually, "Well, why didn't

---

2 *It's totally possible and I absolutely did.*

you just throw the bag away after lunch?"

I stayed silent, without an answer, but wanted to repeat what I'd heard her rhetorically ask a thousand times, in reference to any number of products: "Do you know what those things cost?"

Aside from that, how was I to know at the end of lunch that the bag would fester throughout the afternoon? I had no prior experience of a used paper bag causing issue. Like everything else in my backpack and cubby—the pink erasers and box of crayons and yellow plastic ruler—the brown paper bag was innocuous. I'd never known such things to be capable of harm.

Relief trickled through me the next day when I realized the smell had abated, but from then on I moved about the school, about the world at large, with ever-present anxiety. I wore T-shirts when I played outside in the summertime because I had nipples, and that was bad. I compulsively smelled my possessions to prevent another incident of ruining the school. I feared embarrassment and disgrace and worried the world would learn of my excessive production of saliva (though if that was my superpower, surely there was some way to use it for good, I reasoned).

I still love a good egg salad sandwich. In fact, it doesn't have to be a *good* egg salad sandwich. I'll eat them from triangular plastic containers, prepackaged God knows where and when, and sold in gas stations. To this day, it feels like a guilty pleasure in which I indulge at the expense of others.

Deviled eggs conjure the same memory.

Decades after the egg salad sandwich incident, I found myself living in a rural apartment in Morocco. My husband, Mike, worked inhumane hours as part of a film crew, while I spent my days reading, panicking about my limited number of reading materials, and descending slowly into insanity from extreme isolation. This was before the time of e-books and widespread internet, and the apartment did not have a television. I played enough solitaire that my deck of cards wore down to the texture of tissue. Though I battled boredom and solitude, these were small prices to pay, for how many women in their early twenties luck into such experiences? I was in a foreign land with zero responsibilities. It was like my dream job, without any actual work.

One of my distractions was trying to prepare meals with unfamiliar ingredients in a kitchen that confounded me. I'd never before seen a tagine, nor did I know how to make use of a small grate that rested over coals and was built into a partition wall separating the kitchen from the living room. And by unfamiliar ingredients, I'm speaking of real, whole foods at the small market within walking distance. I never did find the aisle containing the only foods I knew how to make at the time, like mac and cheese from a box or Tuna Helper, also from a box. The culinary skills of my twenties did not venture much beyond overly processed pasta products with packets of sauce powder.

One afternoon, I managed a small batch of deviled eggs. When I finished, pleased with myself, I placed them in the fridge to wait for Mike's return from work. I felt like I'd accomplished something truly great.

A knock at the door startled me. The owners of the apartment, along with the property manager, had stopped by for an impromptu inspection. They wanted to make sure the American film crew, of which we were a part, was not wreaking havoc. I divined this from the sign language the property manager and I used to communicate, along with a few words he spoke in English.

"Owner," he said, pointing to the couple by his side. "Want see apartment."

"Yes," I said, stepping back and beckoning them inside. "*Shokran, shokran.*" The only Arabic I knew was "thanks," and I said this throughout my stay in Morocco, even when it made little sense. You could ask me anything in Arabic—my name, where I was from, if I had any outstanding felony warrants— and my answer would always be "*shokran.*" Thanks!

The apartment was tidy, as we didn't have enough possessions to make it otherwise, but as they entered, I realized just how thick the air was with the stench of boiled egg. Maybe it took the burst of fresh air from outside when I'd opened the door for it to hit me.

"Oh… um… oh," I stammered. The smell engulfed us. The couple wore matching grimaces, so I continued to repeat "Oh… um… oh," interspersed with the occasional *shokran*. I couldn't do the same thing I had done in elementary school. Denial was not an option. There would be no fleeing the scene of the crime. If I suggested that someone had farted, it would had to have been me, as I'd been alone in the apartment.

The odor was so strong that for a moment I imagined it might cause the three Moroccans before me to pass out. Then I could drag their bodies back outside through the front door. They'd regain consciousness, but miraculously not remember the incident at all. And this time when they knocked, I'd hide under the bed and pretend I wasn't home. *This plan is perfect!*

But they only stood before me, expectantly. Not one of them displayed eyes beginning to flutter or roll back into the head. They were staring, clear-eyed and fully present, at me.

I had to find a way to explain, lest they think that this was simply how Americans smelled.

I inhaled dramatically and then exaggerated an expression of disgust, waving my hand in front of my nose.

"*Foo!*" I said, because this is what Russians say when something smells bad. And I didn't speak Arabic, but I spoke Russian, so my mind lurched to find an appropriate foreign word, knowing for once that I couldn't insert my universal *shokran* here. Never mind that my declaration of *foo* made no more sense to them than if I'd gone with "yuck" or "fiddlesticks" or had got down on all fours and begun braying like a donkey.

They stared at me, perplexed. Then I ran to the fridge and retrieved the plate of eggs to show them. *It's not me*, I wanted to say. *It's the eggs! I promise!*

I wasn't sure if I'd gotten my point across, but then a new fear emerged. What if they thought I was giving *them* the eggs? If they took them, we'd be back to our usual fare of tuna on crackers (as close to Tuna Helper as I'd been able to muster). I couldn't risk them taking the eggs. All that work and stench for nothing.

Words and thoughts tumbled in my head: *Foo! Shokran! Is the wife reaching for the plate of eggs? Will I have to wrestle her for them? Double-foo!! Double-shokran!!* I defensively pulled away the plate of eggs and scurried back to the refrigerator.

The owners and property manager chatted in low voices, and suddenly I was six again, fearful and imagining them to be calculating how much I'd have to pay for the ruined apartment. *What if it was worse than that? What would life be like in a Moroccan jail?* I didn't know, but guessed that it wouldn't be an experience I'd describe as "super!" The situation came to a merciful close when they left, likely having realized the futility of logic or basic communication when dealing with me.

A part of me still fears that whenever I consume hard-boiled eggs, in any form, the act will have adverse effects on my surroundings. I'll contaminate the air and all people and objects within reach. I'll infect everything with a sulfurous stench. Worst of all, someone will realize that I'm the problem. I'm what smells bad.

I eat them anyway.

CHAPTER 2
HOW TO GET PUNCHED IN THE FACE

There were three types of students in my elementary school: remedial, normal, and advanced. Everyone knew their place. The words "remedial" and "advanced" were freely thrown about, as common as "alphabet" and "detention," with the clear implication that remedial meant dumb and advanced meant smart. Normal kids were somewhere in the middle; they might rise to become advanced kids or slip back into the remedial group. They had the potential to move in either direction. Rarely did remedial kids climb into the normal group. I was remedial, and I accepted this without distress or protest. *Okay,* I thought. *This is who I am.*

School confounded me. The normal and advanced kids understood what was going on and raised their hands and answered questions, while I felt like everyone around me was speaking in tongues, yet somehow still communicating with one another. My suspicion that I wasn't very bright was confirmed by my stepmother, who matter-of-factly suggested that perhaps I was not very bright.

Because of my lackluster academic performance, I put my greatest efforts into lunch and recess, during which I could trade stickers with other kids. I took my sticker collection seriously, as if I were a first responder to crises. Should anyone find themselves in need of a sticker, I was there at the ready. I was a lot like the character in a movie who is dispatched to disarm a bomb. Only different.

In addition to stickers, I loved the mall. There were few greater outings when I was a child than walking that air-conditioned loop of commerce. It was the chance to covet millions of things we could never afford. If she felt flush (or at least above the poverty line), my mother might let me choose something from the candy kiosk. She'd select a chocolate truffle for herself, while I'd waffle between rock candy or something gelatinous like gummy bears or gummy worms. The form of gummy I'd choose would depend on how cuddly or gross I might be feeling on that particular day.

The mall usually meant a stop at The Wicker Store, which had an actual name other than The Wicker Store, but that's what we called it. They sold wicker furniture, vogue décor at the time, but also all manner of intriguing and exotic treasures, like tiny elephants carved out of marble and miniature gongs and paper lanterns. Perusing The Wicker Store was most enjoyable when I could do so with a bag of gummy bears or worms in hand.

"We're actually just going to stop in at the eye doctor," my mother said as we parked one day near the JCPenney. This was terrifically disappointing. Even sock shopping would have been more exciting than going to the mall to see some form of doctor. There was something suspect about a doctor in a shopping mall. Was that where you went if you'd been shunned by the rest of the medical community?

"Is it going to hurt?" I asked.

Doctors made me think of needles. If anyone came near my eyeballs with a needle, I'd run. I could hide under the carousel racks of clothes in JCPenney. At night I'd sleep in a papasan chair at The Wicker Store and scavenge the candy kiosk for gummy bears. It felt like a workable plan.

"It's not going to hurt," she said, "but you might need glasses."

Smart people in sitcoms wore glasses. Brainy Smurf wore glasses. Scientists wore glasses. Though I'd made peace with my place in the remedial group, my first thought at the mention of glasses was of upward mobility. Glasses would make me smarter, and maybe I would move up to the normal group. Surely glasses would activate dormant parts of my brain. Perhaps I'd not only shed being remedial, but also do something amazing, like cure cancer. It would be extra special because I was still a kid. Someone would probably give me a medal and put my picture in the paper.

We didn't stop at the candy kiosk. Instead, I suffered through my first of many appointments with an optometrist whose breath was rank enough that it compelled me to hold mine. For some reason, it brought mold and old sweaters to mind. He was one of those adults who, along with his halitosis, exuded a dislike of children.

"Cover your left eye," he said. It took me a minute to comply, because I wasn't breathing and was entirely focused on maintaining consciousness.

Two weeks after that first appointment, we returned, and the same doctor, who I could recognize in a lineup simply by asking him to exhale, placed the glasses on my face. I was ready to feel smarter and share with the world my sudden knowledge of the cure for cancer, but nothing happened.

"Well?" my mother asked. "Do they work?"

Both adults stared at me. I wanted to bolt, wanted to do anything I could to evade the doctor's face an inch from my own. *Flee the scene of the crime! Wait, I haven't committed a crime, have I? Other than not being overly bright?*

The optometrist's office shared a wall with the outside, rather than being buried in the bowels of the mall, and one wall included a panel of four cut-out windows. *I'll get a good running start and crash through one of those windows to make my escape, just like they do in the movies. After that,* I thought, *I'll have to live on a lamb, because that's what fugitives do.*

Instead, I quietly mumbled, "Um, yeah, I guess so."

At school, I continued in a fog of existence and only ever answered the teacher's questions with "I don't know."

Because I really didn't know.

Anything.

It turned out that while I didn't know anything, neither did my optometrist, who screwed up my prescription. This was discovered when my teacher mentioned to my mother just how often I'd forget to put on my glasses. I was indifferent to wearing them. Maybe something was wrong with them, she ventured, because if they worked, surely I'd prefer to have them on.

With the error corrected, I was given a second pair of glasses. This time, the fog lifted. Even from afar, trees had leaves, and grass was comprised of individual blades. Most shocking were clouds. While I'd known the details of grass and trees because I could bring my face within an inch of them, as well as touch them, I'd never dreamed of the possible dimension of a cumulonimbus cloud. I could stare at the sky for hours. Doing so felt like hovering on the verge of enlightenment, and only once was I rudely jolted from my euphoria by a bird pooping on my face. And yes, my mouth was partially open at the time.

When I first saw the world around me, my head felt heavy

and hot and pulsed with anger. *I've been duped. My entire life, everyone else has been seeing all of these things! How could they let this happen for seven and a half years?* I wondered. Didn't they know that seven and a half years was a lifetime? Which it was, because that was the extent of my life at that point, and I felt I'd spent it missing out on the world. For all I knew, I could have spent my days thus far solving previously unsolvable crimes, only I'd been cheated from my destiny because I hadn't been able to see the clues in front of me. They'd taken away my chance at being the first female seven and a half-year-old version of Sherlock Holmes! *Bastards*.

Though the world was new, my vision was not a simple fix. My eyesight worsened over time, and by the fifth grade I had bifocals. Today, a kid might have bifocals without anyone else knowing, but this wasn't possible in the early eighties. The lenses themselves were chunky—thick, rectangular hunks with sharply carved half-moons in them.

"What's wrong with your glasses?" kids would ask.

"They're bifocals," I'd explain.

"Those are for old people," they'd say.

Or, "My grandma has those."

The bright side was that, unlike my first pair of glasses, once I received the correct prescription, they *did* make me smarter. I went from remedial to advanced, bypassing normal altogether, from silent student to top nerd.

While I enjoyed knowing that I was not a moron, as many had suspected, I grew tired of constantly having to explain my bifocals and admit that, yes, my glasses were just like the ones for old people.

In my arsenal of stickers (puffy stickers, googly-eyed stickers, Scratch-n-Sniff, you name it), I had a sheet of very small stickers with pictures of random items. It was the sticker equivalent of all the little emojis you might include in a text message. Two of these tiny stickers were eyes.

"Mom?" I asked. "Can I put these stickers on my glasses?" I displayed my find.

"Oh… um… I guess so." If she'd had any doubt up until that point that her daughter was a nerd, I'd surely erased it with my question.

I peeled the tiny eye stickers off of their backing and put one on each of my lenses, in the lower outside corners so they wouldn't interfere with my vision. The lenses were large, providing plenty of real estate with which to work.

My rationale was distraction. People would surely notice the stickers, and then maybe the bifocals themselves would fade from view.

"That's weird," kids said.

"You were four-eyes, and now you're, like, six-eyes," one commented.

Likely this was meant to offend, but I ran with it, embracing this moniker fully. Six-eyes. *Could that be my superhero name?* It was as if I'd found my identity. I didn't wait for other kids to adopt it; I shoved it unceremoniously in their merely two-eyed faces. When a classmate would ask, "What's on your glasses?" I would answer willingly.

"They're little eyeball stickers. So, I used to be four-eyes, but now I'm six-eyes!"

My proclamation was often met with silence.

I could sense in some of them the same hesitation I'd felt from my mother. A part of them wanted to save me from myself, to try to tame my awkwardness for me, guide me into a state that wouldn't necessarily reach cool but at least not be quite so dorky. Once I latched on to something though, it was hard to deter me.

My sticker-clad, Coke-bottle bifocals were one small part of a greater tragedy that included regular haircuts from my mother. It should be noted that my mother had no experience in cutting hair. This, combined with the fashionable mullet style of the day, spelled disaster.

From Bugs Bunny and later Jack Nicholson as the Joker, I learned the line, "You wouldn't hit a guy with glasses, would you?" This seemed less to do with concern for the spectacles and more about the fact that anyone who was unfortunate enough to have to wear glasses was likely not worth the effort. In any case, the idea of refraining from hitting someone because they wear glasses is not universally adopted. Both Bugs Bunny and the Joker immediately took a fist after trying out the glasses plea. My experience occurred in the sixth grade, which is painful enough without getting punched in the face.

By sixth grade, the cool kids openly referred to me as President of the Nerd Convention. At least I got to be president. It wasn't my high office that got me punched in the face, just a random pushing match that escalated into a closed fist.

At the time, teachers would remain in their classrooms with the doors locked until they were ready to face the hordes of middle schoolers waiting for entry. We'd bunch up in hormonal knots outside the doors, eager to get inside the school so we could complain about school. Class was about harassing our teachers and staring longingly at our crush of the moment.

We were clustered in the hallway, a mass of pubescence with our curled bangs and acne and neon-colored clothing and an inexplicable amount of patterns involving triangles, when a boy belligerently pushed his way through the crowd. It was so blatantly rude that I pushed back. He turned to see who was ballsy enough to have pushed him. It was me, President of the Nerd Convention. I was ballsy.

He pushed me again.

I pushed him harder.

I believe at this point, having had a four-push volley, our interchange qualified as an actual fight, at least by middle school standards.

He slapped me, which made it no-going-back official. I threw him against a bank of lockers.

And then he punched me in the face.

It was a good punch, the stunning type. You don't know what to do with yourself in the seconds after being punched in the face. It's like you're falling through the air, helpless for a few moments, just waiting to realize how bad it feels and wondering when you'll get your bearings again. It's like the first time you get the wind knocked out of you or come close to drowning or touch your tongue to another person's tongue. You know your body has experienced a trauma, but you have to get through the shock and confusion before you can really assess what's happened.

I'd never been a fighter. When kids gathered for after-school knockdowns, I never watched eagerly and chanted, "Fight, fight, fight!" When I saw others doing that, it brought tears to my eyes. Something about the mob mentality of it hurt my heart. I'm adversely affected by chaos, an anxiety that has persisted into adulthood. Not only the chaos involving people. I'm equally distressed by the chaos of my husband's closet or desk or the towering pile of random objects he builds by his side of the bed.

Though I didn't like school fights, I loved boxing, so it wasn't the brutality of one person hitting another that disturbed me; it was the chaos of it. No one was there to stop the fight if need be, or ring the bell at the end of a round. Boxing had an elegance and order to it.[3]

The fights that took place in the schoolyard were often between two girls. The leader of the preps versus the leader of the rednecks (we nerds were never invited). They were vicious battles. They pulled hair and raked their nails across each other's faces. I remember two girls attacking each other in a scheduled bout, one grabbing the other violently by the boob and pulling and twisting with all the force she could muster.

When it came to the boys, there were planned group battles. As in, Tuesday after school, the preps and the rednecks were going to fight. These were forecast to be epic rumbles, but for one reason or another they were always called off. I'm not sure if a truce had been reached, or maybe one of the key participants had an orthodontics appointment. In any case, they never happened.

After getting punched in the face, I made one last lunge at my foe and pushed him to the ground. Our fight ended. Teachers intervened, reluctantly emerging from behind their locked doors to march us off to the assistant principal's office.

---

[3] *Until Mike Tyson bit off Evander Holyfield's ear. What was the aftermath of that? Did Holyfield have his ear reconstructed, or does he look in the mirror and get immediately reminded of Mike Tyson gnawing on his face? If it was reconstructed, from where did they harvest spare cartilage? Just enough from the other ear to balance out the two? I have a keen interest in subjects of rearranged facial cartilage.*

It was an intimidating place to be, even for someone with a title like *president*, such as I had.

She asked us questions, like why we would do such a thing, and imparted various wisdoms on all the ways one might better resolve their differences with another. Both my adversary and I cried in that office, and I remember relief and wonder at the fact that the boy was crying too. I never learned his name.

I nervously went back to class, not embarrassed that I'd been in a fight but dismayed that I'd been both slapped and punched while only pushing back, albeit once into a bank of lockers and then to the ground. Why hadn't I responded to his punch in kind? Did I even know how to punch someone? Was I capable of such a thing? What was proper fist form? Where was one to put one's thumb? [4]

In class, I sat next to Thomas Green. He was a cool kid and a clown and a skater and attractive, all at the same time. I'm not sure he'd ever spoken to me before. "Hey," he whispered. "That was a really good fight. You did really good." He looked me in the eye and with sincerity. I may have blushed.

Reassured about my performance, I went through the rest of the day in a good mood. It was the last day of school before a four-day weekend, which I would spend at my father's house. No one at my father's house knew that I was President of the Nerd Convention (though they likely suspected as much). It was a refuge where my father would unapologetically destroy the rest of the family at card games, and my stepmother would cook Martha Stewart recipes and create French country décor with the aid of a hot-glue gun. As we drove to my

---

4 *These questions still linger.*

father's home in a small Virginia town, I told him I'd been in a fight with a boy.

"Did you win?" he asked.

"No," I admitted. I didn't think I'd been beaten. I knew for certain I hadn't won.

The next morning, I woke up and found my glasses broken. Despite the fact that they'd been sitting on a wooden chair next to my bed, I tried to convince myself that Exodor, my dad's hundred-pound mutt, had sat on them. Surely it was Exodor's fault, no matter that Exodor was entirely incapable of sitting on a small wooden chair. My dad suggested that perhaps the frames had cracked during my fight, but I resisted. This notion troubled me.

I had no second pair of glasses. After the four-day weekend, I had to return to school with tape holding my broken frames together.

Oh, the horror.

There could be no clearer sign of the epitome of uncool than having tape hold your glasses together. I'd gone beyond average nerd and become a parody of myself.

"Hey, you the girl that was in that fight?"

I was huddled with the masses outside the school doors, waiting to be let in. It seemed the teachers loved locking us out and waiting to let us in. They must have relished those moments. The air was frigid. I turned to my left to see two girls standing there, the one who'd posed the question and a more timid sidekick.

"Yeah," I confirmed. "That was me."

"He break your glasses?"

"What? No," I said. "No, my dad's dog sat on them." Even as I said the words, I cursed myself for not coming up with a more plausible alternate reality.

"Mmm hmm." She nodded doubtfully, then turned to her minion. "He broke her glasses when he punched her in the face." She looked pleased by this and hurried off excitedly, sidekick following behind. I realized then that while I had Thomas Green telling me I'd done okay, my opponent had his own corner person, who would gleefully report that I was suffering further ramifications of his fist to my face.

The embarrassment of spending the next week and a half with tape holding my glasses together was incandescent in nature, a pain far more intense and lasting than getting punched in the face. I'd embraced the identity of Six Eyes (true superhero names deserve to be capitalized) because it was something I'd chosen. I'd taken control of my situation. The tape, on the other hand, was evidence that I'd not been in control, that something had been done to me against my will. It was a sign of weakness. And middle school, as we all know, is difficult to survive with outward signs of weakness. Because the tape was squarely between my eyeballs, it was impossible for anyone to look at me without acknowledging its presence.

Why had I taped my glasses together when I could have asked my stepmother to employ her hot-glue gun skills? Was it because I was used to the sitcom image of nerds with tape on their glasses and simply fell into the role? The hot-glue gun could have fused the crack in the bridge of my plastic frames and eliminated considerable angst.

On some level, I knew that the sitcom character who existed for comic relief was me. That would always be my role. I was the kid with tape on her glasses, and I'd take that any day over returning to a silent, remedial existence. I collected pocket protectors and begged my mother for a filing cabinet. While other kids contemplated shoplifting candy, I was eyeing the mechanical pencils. Maybe I wore that tape on my glasses like a badge of honor. It was a clear declaration of who I was—a nerd who got in fights, yes, but also someone who could finally see, and participate in, the world at large.

CHAPTER 3
MOTHERLAND

Though I accepted my nerdiness as a child, I wasn't yet ready to abandon all hope of becoming cool. It seemed to me that they didn't need to be mutually exclusive. Maybe being cool was something I should keep striving for. Perhaps I could learn it or catch it from one of the cool kids. You could get mono and STDs from the cool kids, so why couldn't a little of their coolness be transmitted as well?

Unable to catch any level of cool, or a case of gonorrhea, from the cool kids, I instead turned my focus to my future self. What could I *do* that was cool?

Rock stars were cool. Unfortunately, I have no rhythm and I'm tone deaf. These presented as substantial barriers to becoming a rock star. There are exceptions, of course, including many musical artists whom I appreciate. Neil Young and Bob Dylan come to mind. Like animals that are so ugly they somehow become cute—*because* of how ugly they are. I knew I was not capable of such feats.

Abandoning the idea of rock star, I looked elsewhere. I also thought that spies were cool, and it seemed to me that nerds could be spies. They weren't automatically excluded, because everyone knew that the intelligence community could greatly benefit from the intelligence of nerds.

When I grew up, Roger Moore (handsome in that truly classical, early-seventies kind of way) was James Bond, and in the movies, he traveled around, spying and drinking and womanizing and spying. Surely that was something I could do, minus the womanizing. I watched *The Spy Who Loved Me* ad nauseum, reasoning that it was research for my future life in espionage.[5]

As I entered puberty and the Cold War thawed, an opportunity presented itself. My middle school ran a pilot program that offered Russian. They weren't sure if the program would continue after that first year. They made it clear that the availability of any future Russian language classes would be dependent on interest. In reality, I think they stumbled across a Russian teacher and figured they might as well give her a shot. Either way, I was interested. Russian. It sounded so exotic. I didn't know any Russians. No one I knew did either.

According to most of the movies at the time, Russia was comprised of soldiers who were always soldiering, and boxer Ivan Drago, who really wanted to beat up Rocky. They were also the chief bad guys in *Red Dawn*. Total assholes. Was there more to Russia? No one knew for sure. During Soviet rule, there

---

5 *One summer, I babysat two kids for a single mom who worked as a nurse. The job began at 4 a.m. Most days, I'd arrive and sleep on the couch until the kids woke. On days I couldn't go back to sleep, I'd rifle through her VHS collection, which included* The Spy Who Loved Me. *Twice the kids woke before me and got into trouble, once drawing on the walls of their bedroom, another time raiding their mom's bathroom. When my employer came home that afternoon, I showed her the chaos, including dismantled tampons and her vibrator, which I'd been afraid to touch. It was the first time I'd seen a vibrator, though I was old enough to know that's what it was. My employer's shame at seeing her pleasure device out there in the open could not have been more tangible. Without looking at me, she whispered, "You can go now."*

wasn't much travel back and forth between Russia and America. No one vacationed in Leningrad; they went to Palm Springs.[6]

Long before the globalization of travel for the privileged, Russians and the language they spoke were thought of with intrigue and suspicion. I wanted to be intriguing and suspicious, so in my mind, that made it a perfect fit. So, in the seventh grade, I came home from school one day and announced to my mother that I was going to learn to speak Russian and become an international spy. She said okay.

It turned out that I had an aptitude for languages. I could pick them up fairly easy, and my pronunciation was spot-on. This started early in childhood when I would copy my sister, who could speak in a range of accents and characters, from British royalty to the girlfriend of a Colombian drug dealer. It seemed unfair that I could mimic the foreign sounds of other languages but couldn't sing a song on key, even if my guinea pig's life had depended on it. I'd never be a rock star, but I thrived in Russian class. As well, there were enough students to keep the program going, and the Russian teacher decided to stick around.

By the time I was fifteen, I had a few years of Russian in me and a chunk of cash[7] I'd saved up to put toward a study-abroad program. I told my mom I wanted to go live in Russia

---

6 *Years later, after the fall of the Soviet Union, when Leningrad was no longer Leningrad because they changed it back to St. Petersburg (which might soon change again because I wouldn't be surprised if Putin declares it Putinsville or maybe Putopia), my husband and I went to Palm Springs. It was filled with Russians.*

7 *The cash came from a patchwork of part-time jobs, from the aforementioned babysitting to Baskin Robbins to shoveling manure on a rural farm in West Virginia.*

for four months. Again, she said okay.

The host family in whose care I was placed lived in a suburb of Moscow. The apartment was typical of Eastern Europe: small kitchen with a mini-fridge, random walls decorated with murals of birch forests, clothes-drying rack off the living room window where you could freeze your clothing into wearable icicles in the winter.

The family was highly dysfunctional. I guess every family is dysfunctional to some extent, but a family's dysfunction becomes shockingly apparent when you move in with them. One of the main problems, as I saw it, was that the family included three generations living in a two-bedroom, one-bath apartment. That was a pretty common living scenario (actually, this is a familiar setup in much of the world—but in America, we like everything big, from our sodas to our personal space, and we've perfected the art of shipping off the elderly to care facilities). The problem with my Russian host family was that on top of such close quarters, they didn't appear to like one another. Throw a fifteen-year-old American outsider in the mix, and the result was a shocking level of discomfort. The tension in that apartment was thick enough that it made the air hard to breathe, like trying to inhale chocolate pudding. Don't get me wrong; I love chocolate pudding, but I don't want it in my lungs.

There was one ray of sunshine in that apartment. The grandmother.

Note: grandmother in Russian is *BAH-booshka*. You have to really put emphasis on and draw out that first syllable. As if you were a sheep. The word is often mispronounced as *bah-BOOshka*. And that means scarf. Don't call your grandmother a scarf.

Babushka reached about four feet tall, but she was thick.

Not fat but solid, in that she could probably bench-press great weights if she had been so inclined. She walked as if her joints were fused together, as if she didn't have the capability of moving her shoulders or hips. Sort of like how you'd play with a plastic green army soldier, pivoting back and forth from leg to leg to mimic real human movement. When she smiled, light glinted off half a dozen silver teeth interspersed in her mouth. The first time I saw this, I was taken aback. Ironically—or perhaps appropriately—it reminded me of the character Jaws,[8] the bad guy from *The Spy Who Loved Me*. Wispy gray curls swirled around Babushka's head. Her wardrobe consisted of shapeless, drab dresses and slippers. She was a kick in the pants.

Babushka spoke no English. And while I'd been a whiz in the Russian classroom back in America, I was quite far from being able to communicate fluidly with a native Russian speaker. It didn't matter. She had kind eyes and always greeted me with that silver smile.

The prospect of attending school in Russia was thrilling, an escape from the stifling tension of the apartment, the chance to interact with people. Attending school meant a lot of smiling and nodding, pretending that I knew what was going on around me. In a way, it felt like a throwback to my early elementary days before glasses. Instead of an inability to see anything around me, this time I had the inability to understand the words being spoken. As my conversational Russian improved toward

_____

[8] *Played by Richard Kiel, who apparently could only wear the dental insert that looked like steel-capped teeth for a minute or so before it made him gag. Incidentally, Kiel and I both once worked as door-to-door vacuum cleaner salespeople. So, you know, there's that.*

fluency throughout the trip, I still remained in a fog in the classroom. Physics in your native language is hard enough. I had no chance of gaining a scientific vocabulary, much less applying it and actually learning something. I'll leave physics, in any language, to the physicians.[9]

When the first day of school rolled around, I had my outfit all picked out. A white blouse and a red, pleated skirt. Babushka asked what I'd be wearing and nodded appreciatively when I showed her. Why she didn't take that moment to tell me that all the other children would be dressed in black and white, and that my red skirt would stand out like the lipstick stains on my host father's collar after returning from a "business trip," I'll never know. Or maybe she did tell me, but I didn't understand. In any case, Babushka took my blouse and skirt, saying she would have them ready for me for the first day of school. When the morning came, Babushka returned my freshly ironed blouse to me, along with my no-longer-pleated skirt. She'd been confused by the pleats and had attempted to iron them out, thinking them to be wrinkles that were oddly symmetrical, uniform, and deep.

Returning to the apartment after school put me on edge. Who would be home? The mother always appeared on the verge of tears, because she was constantly belittled by her husband and daughter. That same daughter was entirely fluent in English but refused to speak to me, preferring to communicate with only sneers and daggers shot from her eyes. She hated me for many reasons, including the fact that I was given her bedroom and I made out with a boy for whom she had unabashed and unrequited love. This occurred

---

9   *Wait, that's not right.*

during an unsupervised party at the family's *dacha* (cabin), where no one seemed concerned with the lack of drinking water, because vodka. Incidentally, that same boy with whom I made out (because vodka) was betrothed to her younger sister, who was studying in the US while I was studying in Russia. It's complicated but also makes sense. Under normal circumstances such a miserable family wouldn't want to add another person into the mix. They did so only because they received money for taking me in, which helped offset the costs of sending their youngest daughter abroad.

The days when I returned to find only Babushka at home were glorious. She'd make a stack of *blini*, thin Russian pancakes that we'd fold over and dip in butter,[10] and the two of us would watch reruns of *Santa Barbara*.

At the time, all American movies had voice-overs by the same Russian man. He did voice-overs for all roles, with no attempt at differentiation or inflection. No matter who spoke, their words were repeated in the same monotone drone. This was true for *Santa Barbara* and for the handful of movies they had on VHS. Sadly, there were no spy movies. With the exception of Rambo, the VHS tapes all displayed an obsession with Julia Roberts. As a result, I've seen *Pretty Woman*, *Mystic Pizza*, and *Sleeping with the Enemy*, all dubbed in Russian, more than the recommended dose.

In Russia, I made friends with two groups of teenagers. One group was comprised of three girls. These were good girls and good friends, polite, smart, sober, and optimistic. The other group had the teens who smoked and drank in the

---

10 *Upon my return to America, I was notably plumper than I'd been before the trip.*

underground basements (think glorified crawlspaces) of the mammoth apartment buildings that loomed overhead. As it turned out, I kind of liked hanging out with the bad crowd. I liked the good girls too, but the experience taught me that I was just as inclined toward ruffians as I was to saints. That's fairly normal when you drop a teenager into a foreign country with no adult supervision. I learned a lot during that time, including things like drinking and smoking and that there are people in the world who believe your ovaries will freeze if you sit on cold concrete.

When my study abroad came to an end and it was time to leave, I cried. Despite my host family, I'd come to love the rows of drab gray buildings and speaking Russian every day and venturing into Moscow on my own. The independence made me feel adult, perhaps before I should have. Which is not to say that I was overly supervised during my life back in America. I was a Gen X latchkey kid whose mother placed in her an illogical amount of trust. Nevertheless, four months of autonomy in the Motherland was like a drug I didn't want to quit. I had fleeting thoughts of staying, of simply not returning to America. I was sixteen by that point and thought that surely I could find some sort of work, just by virtue of the fact that I was fluent in English. I'd live in an apartment in Moscow and build a life there. The plan was about as viable as my childhood notion of escaping a torturous optometrist by hiding in clothing racks and living on the lam at our local shopping mall. I realized this and returned to the US. I'm pretty sure it was the right move.

Back in America, I continued my Russian studies, breezing through language classes and intimidating the new Russian teacher who'd been hired at my high school. She was a timid, birdlike woman to begin with, and though her Russian was far better than mine when it came to important things like grammar and vocabulary, I *sounded* more like a Russian. My accent was good, and I had an impressive command of Russian slang and obscenities.

The second time I went to Russia was four years later, this time living in a dormitory instead of with a dysfunctional family. I made no attempt to contact my hosts from four years prior, though I did wonder if Babushka was still in good health and still watching *Santa Barbara*. And had they added *The Pelican Brief*, one of Julia Roberts's movies that had come out in the interim, to their VHS collection?

I made contact with my friends from that first trip. The good girls picked me up from the airport, and the ruffian crowd had grown even more ruffian than before. The biggest change I noted in my four-year absence was the difference in the city itself. Moscow had exploded, going from its communism hangover to full-blown capitalism and becoming the second most expensive city in the world.

I studied Russian at Moscow State University and drank vodka and survived on instant noodles I made in my dorm room. At some point during that trip, I came to terms with the fact that I didn't want to be a spy after all. I let go of any belief that intelligence work would be anything like it was in the movies. As well, Moscow no longer filled me with the same sense of wonder that it did four years prior. It was cosmopolitan and teemed with beautiful-looking people. What happened to all the endearing, four-foot grandmothers with silver teeth and head scarves?

The only work that I ever ended up doing with my Russian degree was freelance tutoring of the Russian language. And the only students I ever had were old men, trying to learn a few phrases in Russian before their mail-order brides came to the US. It was the most depressing work I've ever done and left me wanting a shower, because I felt like an instrument of the sex trade.

There was one family I'll never forget. The man was in his sixties, pale, plump, and pockmarked. His Russian wife was in her early thirties, shockingly pretty and effortlessly elegant, and came with a ten-year-old daughter. The daughter was the only one of the three who was bilingual and therefore could serve as the tool of communication between her mother and stepfather, but she recoiled at the suggestion of this role, just as my host sister in Moscow had opted out of serving as translator for me. The ten-year-old was old enough to see the situation for what it was and knew that she was part of the price her stepfather paid for his mail-order bride.

Somehow, I became connected with this family, ostensibly to serve in a sort of big-sister role to the little girl. This proved disastrous for many reasons. The reality of the situation itself was ill-fated, for starters. A man who wanted sex. A woman who wanted a better life for her daughter. And a daughter who knew all of this. It was toxic all around. I lost touch with them, for which I'm thankful, but I'll always wonder what happened to them and can't help but reflect with a pang of regret. Part of me feels like I failed that little girl, but I also know she needed therapy more than a twenty-something bartender who happened to speak her native language. The last time I heard from her, she left eleven messages on my answering machine in the span of half an hour, irate that I wasn't answering her call. She wanted to know when Mike and I would be coming over for dinner again. We'd been once, and at the end of the evening I immediately promised Mike I'd never again subject him to such an experience. But that's what you do when you're in your early twenties and have no kids and suck at saying no to things you don't want to do. You agree to dinner invitations in the most uncomfortable of circumstances.

I'm not sure how long we were actually in their apartment, but it felt equivalent to back-to-back showings of every *Matrix*, *Lord of the Rings*, *Star Wars*, and *Harry Potter* movie ever made. As soon as we walked in, the three members of their doomed family began talking at me at once, two of them in Russian, one in English. The ten-year-old wanted to vent, the mother wanted a friend, and the father wanted to tell me about his thriller manuscript which, once in the hands of the right people, would change everything and allow him to quit his job as a used car salesman. It was the type of situation in which you attempt to make polite conversation while simultaneously calculating how many seconds[11] you have yet to endure before you're released back into freedom.

In all honesty, I didn't promise Mike I'd never again subject him to that painful experience. I think what actually happened was that, upon saying our goodbyes and getting back into our car, he said, "I am never doing that again." There was no room to doubt his meaning or conviction.

After college, I had a degree in Russian but decided that I instead wanted to be a writer. And I'd write in English, of course. I had no idea what I wanted to write, so the first thing that came to mind was The Great American Novel. But when I thought about it, that seemed terribly difficult. Mike suggested I write horror, because he was used to me

---

[11] *Sixty seconds per minute x 60 minutes per hour x approximately 2 hours = 7,200 yet to endure.*

sharing my nightmares with him.

I dreamed often of things like bears, but it wasn't your typical nightmare of being chased by bears—more like my job was to go around town and find all the bears and slit their throats. Okay, I know that probably paints the picture of me being a genuine sicko, but the bear dreams only started after I met Mike and heard a million bear stories from his years growing up in Alaska. So the sicko stuff all really originated with him.

"You dreamed that?" he asked after I related the gory details, the look on his face indicating that he was rethinking our relationship.

"Well, yeah, but it's not like I chose to dream it."

"True," he conceded, "but…" His dismay at the fact that his wife's brain held such thoughts and images, even if not consciously, went unsaid. Sadly, I can't blame him (or at least haven't yet figured out how to) for my other nightmares, like the more garden variety ones involving serial killers or undercooked pork products or running out of wood floor cleaner or, worse, the most terrifying of all, a nightmare involving all of the aforementioned elements.

When you decide you want to be a writer, your next step should be to sit down and write, but more often than not, you instead begin looking for waitressing jobs. Because that's what a lot of artists do; they start out spending a solid decade waiting tables and scrubbing toilets. There are other possibilities during this time, but the general consensus is that the work should somehow relate to another's consumption or elimination. So, waiting tables and scrubbing toilets fits the bill on both counts. Art unfortunately doesn't always pay to keep the lights on or, let's be honest, cover the bar tab. As a result of my decade of waiting tables and scrubbing toilets,[12] I am a fantastic tipper and always leave a restroom cleaner than I found it. I'm the person who takes a paper towel and wipes down all the sinks before I leave a public bathroom. This seems like a good thing, unless you have to live with me, in which case I'm just annoyingly obsessive.

I wasn't living completely like a starving artist in the post-college years. Mike is an incredibly patient and indulgent husband who has always been better at making money than I am. We suffered through some excruciatingly poor years in the beginning but have since managed to eke out a solid middle-class living. Mike is business-minded, logical, and driven, but I'm a better speller, so there's that. He's tolerant of the fact that writers don't make much money,[13] and he's ridiculously attractive. There should be some major flaw to balance all of this out, like a third arm sprouting from the middle of his back or a secret life in which he sneaks off to do unspeakable things, like slosh water all over the sinks of public restrooms, but I haven't discovered anything of the sort as of yet.

I met my husband both because of and in spite of the fact that I speak Russian.

Because of: when I was in Russia the second time, I became

---

[12] *It should be noted that these two tasks never occurred in the course of a singular job. I promise that they were always separate endeavors. Just as consumption and elimination should be separate endeavors.*

[13] *Most of the time, writers don't make any money. And if I'm truly being honest, for many of us, it actually costs us money to be writers. So if you're toying with going into the arts, don't do it for the money.*

friends with a woman who would eventually introduce me to the Turner family, into which I'd marry.

In spite of: when Mike first encountered me, I was speaking with that woman, and because we'd met as exchange students in Russia, we often spoke in Russian. As such, the first time he met me, he was told I was "Melissa's friend from Russia." He assumed I was Russian, didn't speak English, and was therefore not someone with whom he could strike up a conversation. Eventually, this error in knowledge would be corrected, and we got on track to lifelong marital bliss.

Someday I'd like to return to the Motherland, maybe to Moscow but more likely to Saint Petersburg, which will hopefully not by that time have been renamed Saint Putinsburg. I can't say I'm not disappointed with what's happened in Russia since my first visit in the early nineties. Fresh off of communism, there was an air of possibility and promise. Who knew where the country might go? And while great things have happened, they've also backpedaled under Putin in certain areas, like basic human rights. Being human, I find that I'm generally a fan of human rights.[14] And on the whole, Russia is kind of a dick to its gay population, which is unfortunate. I've loosely followed Russian news and politics since then. A few years ago, the Russian group Pussy Riot came to Boise. This is not a battle of vaginas but rather a music and performance art group focused on feminism and protesting human rights violations. Pussy Riot made international news when a few band members were imprisoned for things like "hooliganism." As far as I can tell, when Putin arrests someone for hooliganism,

---

14 *Putin's invasion of Ukraine occurred after this essay was written, just prior to publication. I don't yet have words.*

it's his way of saying: 1) get off my lawn; 2) stop denying that I have a huge penis; and 3) real women should be barefoot and pregnant and fixing me some *blini*, all rolled into one.

When Pussy Riot came to town, I thought briefly that maybe I should attend their concert. It would actively demonstrate my dismay at human rights violations. But then I remembered that I don't like crowds or loud music or staying up past 9:30, and it's not like there'd be a discussion on how to mobilize humanitarian efforts, so it was better if I just stayed home, which was exactly what I did. My protesting is far more effective when put to use in other ways.

Whenever I feel nostalgic for my early dreams of spying and drinking and spying (without the womanizing), I can always indulge in the ridiculous amount of media that still thrives on the public's fascination with counterintelligence.[15] Spy movies and novels have not waned in the slightest since Ian Fleming brought James Bond to life on the page in 1953, and Sean Connery brought him to the screen in 1962. The amount of material out there makes me think that I can't be the only one who grew up with this fixation.

Despite my 547 viewings of *The Spy Who Loved Me* and at one point becoming fluent in Russian (I've since forgotten most of it but retain enough to occasionally eavesdrop on someone at the airport or in the grocery store), I never became a spy[16] and to this day remain only a nerd. It's my true calling.

ö Ö ö

---

[15] *This is an odd word. Shouldn't it mean... unintelligence?*
[16] *Or did I...?*

CHAPTER 4
TRUE LOVE STORY [17]

"Go ahead, you two," my mother urged. "Try it out."

I stood with my mother and Mike in the middle of a mattress store. There was so much I still didn't know about him, yet there we were bed shopping. The three of us hovered over a cheaper model, and my mother encouraged us to test it, the mass of springs and fabric that touted spinal health and promised not to go up in flames, at least not quickly, should a fire break out.

Shopping with my mother and boyfriend for a mattress was not a situation I'd ever anticipated. Mike and I looked at the pristine, white rectangle with its faint paisley imprint and felt a collective shame for all that would eventually take place on this bed. Despite my mother's encouragement, the feeling remained—that awkward, giddy embarrassment of blushes

_____

[17] *This essay first appeared in the anthology* I Just Want to Be Alone, *which is a collection of humorous essays by Some Super Cool Lady Writers. I'm not joking; you can look it up. The collection was published in 2014 by @throat_punch Books. If you're thinking to yourself,* Hmm, throat punch… that's both catchy and familiar!, *you're correctly thinking of Jen Mann,* New York Times *bestselling author of the* People I Want to Punch in the Throat *series. It should be noted that I've never actually known Jen to punch someone in the throat. It's possible she may have kneed someone in the balls before, but if she did, it was surely in the name of justice.*

that accompany such a purchase in the presence of a parent. We had every intention of living in sin.

I was twenty-one, Mike was twenty, and my mother had met him twelve hours earlier. I was thankful for her blessing, evidenced by her support of mattress testing, despite the fact that she hardly knew him. He was young and strong and good-looking, but almost too much so, the kind of good-looking that makes you anticipate a person will be an asshole. He had the muscled arms and perfect bone structure of a handsome-but-jerky captain of the football team from an after-school special, and I secretly harbored the fear that he hid a gross defect of character. What if he tortured small animals or had affairs with men in gas stations or was the type of guy who peed all over the toilet seat? I was already in love with him, so there was no turning back. But I really hoped he wouldn't pee all over the toilet seat.

I'd met him three months earlier on a ten-day vacation in Mexico, where we were free from the responsibilities of work and school and US laws on public drunkenness. Meeting someone on vacation tends to speed up the dating process. Instead of meeting once a week for dinner or a movie, you eat all your meals together and wake up together, looking at each other with mirrored expressions of confusion and tentative utterances of "Did we…?"

Mike was vacationing with his family, and on more than one morning of our ten days in Mexico, I'd had to exit his room and pass through the condo kitchen with my eyes on the floor, under the scrutiny of his mother as she made coffee. Twenty years later, she still relishes telling the stories of my walks of shame.

When the vacation ended, we said goodbye in the

airport. Without warning, my emotions rudely took control of my body and reduced me to a puddle of snot and tears, which was certainly not what I wanted as Mike's last image of me. His parents were there that day, and as Mike boarded his plane, I cried on his mother's shoulder while his father, completely befuddled as to how to handle such a situation, feigned sudden enthrallment with a Mexican soap opera on a nearby monitor.

We spent three months pining and hundreds of dollars on phone bills before I decided to pack up my electric-blue Volkswagen Rabbit and travel from Maryland to California to be with him. He was in his first year of college. I was in my last. We agreed that if one of us was going to move, it would be me.

"*How* long were you two in Mexico together?" my mother asked when I told her I was moving.

"Ten days."

"And you want to drive across the country and move in with him?"

"Yes," I confirmed.

I knew that my family might think my decision indicated insanity, drugs, or pregnancy. I held my breath for my mother's reaction.

"Okay," she said. "Want me to drive with you?"

Two weeks later, I pulled up to her house and loaded her tiny suitcase, all that I would permit her, into my packed Volkswagen. She held a newspaper in hand as she opened the passenger side door.

"What's that?" I questioned, motioning to the newspaper.

"What's what?"

"In your hand," I demanded.

"It's a newspaper."

"Yeah, you can't bring that."

"What are you talking about?" She looked confused.

"Sorry, there's just no room."

"No room for my newspaper?"

"You'll have to leave that here."

"I'll just keep it on my lap," she protested.

"You can't," I explained. "I already have your lap items designated."

Lucky for me, my mother was a sport, and after three thousand forty-seven miles and days spent surviving on gas station food, we arrived in a tiny, coastal California town.

"Should we pick up a pizza?" I asked.

"Don't you want to go straight there to see him?" my mother questioned. "You're not getting cold feet, are you?"

"No," I answered. "He's at a crew competition in some other town. He won't be back until tomorrow."

"In that case," she said, "I'd rather find a liquor store."

"Jackpot." I pulled into a strip mall that offered both Little Caesars and liquor. After the week of Pringles and Diet Coke, it felt like fine dining.

"I'll buy these," my mother said in the liquor store, holding up one each of the largest available bottles of gin and vodka. "Consider it a housewarming present."

"Aw, thanks, Mom."

We pulled into the apartment complex long after dark but well before midnight. Balancing pizza and booze, we left the car packed with my possessions and went searching in the dark for the apartment number Mike had given me. I felt a bit like a prowler, but carrying booze made it seem like I was a prowler bearing gifts, which wasn't quite so creepy.

Standing outside the apartment door in California, I knocked because that's what doors ask of me. I followed this with a kick at the doormat where he'd agreed to hide a key. The doormat slid to the side easily, revealing no key underneath. For a brief but heavy moment, I wondered if I was the victim of the most elaborate and cruel prank ever conceived. Get a girl to fall for you, so much so that she quits her job, gives up her apartment, leaves the state during her last semester of college, and drags her mother across the country to meet Mr. Wonderful, who really lives somewhere else entirely and engages in this sadism because he gets off on it. *Fucker.*

But then the door opened.

Mike stood before us, eyes narrowed with sleep and standing in only his boxer shorts. I wondered what my mother would think. Would she purse her lips in disapproval? What if part of his package was hanging out and he didn't know it? *Please let his penis be in place,* I thought. I checked, and all seemed tidily confined, no errant testicle peeking out from bunched-up boxers. I looked to my mother for her reaction. She beamed.

"Hi," Mike said, looking stunned but pleased. "I thought you wouldn't be here until tomorrow."

"And I thought you were on a crew trip."

"Come in," he said and stepped back.

We entered the apartment, suddenly full of awkward tension. My mother and I headed straight for the kitchen to set down the pizza and booze.

"Mom," I said, "this is Mike. Mike, this is my mother, Edie."

"Hi, Edie." He smiled.

"Hi, Mike." She continued to beam.

"Maybe you should go put some clothes on," I suggested, embarrassed that the full hotness of the man I was moving in with was right there on display for his first meeting with my mom.

"He's fine," she chided. "Leave him alone."

"Oh, sorry. I'll be right back," said Mike, ducking out of the kitchen to search for clothes.

As soon as he was out of earshot, my mom turned into a teenager. "Oh my God, he's *so* cute. Did you see the way he *looked* at you?" Then, in a lower voice, "What am I doing here? This should be your moment. I feel like an *intruder*."

We emptied the Volkswagen of my random possessions that seemed worthless but managed to occupy the entire vehicle. Clothes, silverware, toiletries, a framed poster of Billie Holiday, a hammer, a lamp. I'd had my books shipped ahead of time. Just as his athletic activities seemed alien to me, for I'd never before known someone who rowed on a crew team, so did my attachment to books to him.

We had a drink and ate pizza and attempted to relax. And then it was time to go to bed, which was ironically anything but relaxing. We had no beds. Mike's furniture consisted of a lone bookshelf. He'd moved into the apartment from a dorm room, just in time for my arrival. The bookshelf, combined with my lamp, hammer, poster, and spoons, did little to flesh out the place. He had two thin camping pads. We gave the thicker of the two to my mother and took the remaining camping pad and placed it on the carpet in the middle of a bare bedroom. We slept in a prolonged hug while clothed, the sleep of two people who love but hardly know each other, in a room just a wall away from my mother.

The next morning, the three of us set out on a shopping

trip. We bought pots and pans at Goodwill, and I couldn't help but wonder about the undoubtedly dead people whose cookware I was inheriting for a dollar thirty-five apiece. *Hopefully none of them died of Teflon poisoning,* I thought.

At Target, we picked out bedding and random objects like a trash can for the bathroom. I eyed a scale and debated buying it. A woman walked by and said, "Honey, don't do that to yourself." I returned the scale to its shelf.

We went to a mattress store because I didn't think I could take another night pretending that a camping pad on carpet was comfortable, and because we were now the proud new owners of bedding but no bed to put it on. My mom would be forced to tough it out on the camping pad for two more nights before flying back to the East Coast.

Buying a mattress with your brand-new, I-hardly-know-you-and-really-hope-this-works-out, wait-what-the-fuck-are-we-doing significant other is… awkward. Throwing my mother into the mix did nothing to lessen the discomfort of the situation.

"Go ahead, you two," she said, motioning to the low-end queen. "Try it out."

Mike and I looked at each other and then tentatively lay down on the mattress, a prudish foot of space between us, both of us stock straight with arms tucked in tight at our sides. The fluorescent lights of the mattress store seemed to highlight the reality of our moving in together. My mother stood off to the side, smiling in an ill-fated attempt to put us at ease.

She turned away from us, pretending to be interested in a nearby pillow top, which gave me the sudden urge to run and hug her. Instead, I lay still, feeling the energy of lying next to a man on a mattress *we* would buy *together.* While staring at the ceiling, and without a word, our hands met in the space between us.

"This could work," he said.

I wasn't sure if he meant the mattress or us. Either way, I agreed. "Let's try it out."

"Wait," he whispered. "*Here?*"

ö Ö ö

CHAPTER 5
OFF-WHITE [18]

I'm not the frilly sort.

I'm bling-free in a sparkly world.

I do not own a set of pearls.

The first dress I bought was a hot little number. White, simple, short, tight. *If I'm going to suddenly believe in marriage,* I reasoned, *I might as well also believe that this dress is appropriate.* It was not. On ginger toes, my mother offered a shopping trip.

"I won't go to a bridal shop," I vowed. "I don't want a *wedding* dress."

"I know," she said. "I'm your mother."

She herded me to the mall, to a store I don't remember, which probably morphed into a food court addition or cell phone retailer a decade ago. There was the dress. Found, affordable, agreeable, done. It was elegant, a touch of class to counter my tattoos and Marlboros.

We could have forgone the elegance if we'd eloped as planned, but we stupidly publicized our Vegas itinerary.

---

[18] *A year and a half after the events of "True Love Story" came the events of "Off-White." This essay was first published in* Little White Dress *(Mill Park Publishing, 2011). This anthology was put together by Liza Long, author of* The Price of Silence, *and Elaine Ambrose, who has written many funny books, including* Midlife Cabernet, *but is perhaps best known for a viral blog post about how she once farted during an MRI.*

My in-laws pleaded. And triumphed.

Instead: we took a car to a plane to Alaska, to a boat to an island, to wed. Intermixed with thanks to my groom's parents for handling the logistics were my demands of no guests and no God. My wishes were honored.

On a privately-owned island off of Sitka, Alaska, we gathered with parents. Siblings have yet to forgive us the exclusion, but just as I didn't want a real wedding dress, I also didn't want a real wedding.

Mike and I dressed together in the bathroom of an exquisite cabin. Inadvertent elbows took up the tiny room. He zipped me up.

"Isn't there something about the groom not seeing the bride in her dress before the wedding?" he asked.

"Yeah," I answered, "but I don't believe in that crap."

"I love you."

"I love you too."

He wore suspenders, as I requested. I thought they were handsome. In our wedding pictures, we look Amish.

A woman we'd never met before spoke. We repeated words, giddy and light and desperately trying not to mess up our lines. I was twenty-two. He was twenty-one. We were young and stupid and miraculously lucky—still married in love and lust decades later.

Hot little number did not go to waste. I wore it at our in-lieu-of-reception keg party the following day. I wore the wedding dress again on our first anniversary. I tried it on ten minutes ago. It fits, though the body underneath is child-weary.

I'm not the sentimental type.

I own no lace or veil.

I'm keeping the dress.

ö Ö ö

CHAPTER 6
THE DELICATE ARTS OF PURGING AND HOARDING

With all that love and marriage stuff, by my early twenties, I had a husband, home, and dog. Almost like a real adult.

Our first home had a large deck with a lovely view extending out over a picturesque California town in which we couldn't afford to live. The deck sloped menacingly and threatened to fall into a pile of rotting wood at any moment, particularly when one was standing on it. This precarious state of construction detracted from the view because you couldn't look to the horizon without wondering if you were going to plummet to your death while doing so. But that's how poor young people become homeowners; they buy homes that are falling apart or come with things like roach infestations, toxic mold, attic-dwelling opossums, and neighbors who are serial killers.

If we'd had many friends at the time when we owned that first home and its death trap deck, we would likely have been one of those terrible headlines: "22 People Perish as Deck Collapses at House Party." Fortunately for everyone, we had few friends, nowhere close to twenty-two of them. I guess, of the friends we did have, their collective weight was not enough to bring down the deck.

Mike and I committed to improving the home as best we could. We bought how-to books at Home Depot, forgot to turn breakers off while doing electrical work, and spray-painted the front cover of an avocado-green dishwasher to make it look like stainless steel. That last one didn't really work. It looked less like stainless steel and more like someone had spray-painted the front cover of an avocado-green dishwasher.

Painting was a great way to quickly improve the interior of the home. First, we had to remove a substantial amount of wallpaper. It was a godawful job that, for some reason, I found enjoyable. It's godawful because it's sticky and messy like a toddler's birthday party, but enjoyable once you've removed enough wallpaper that your home no longer resembles the living room of your great-grandparents when they were in their prime. It's tedious work, because for some reason, there are sections where the wallpaper only gives up the ghost in tiny increments, but at other times, you can get a huge swath to give way at once, and then you feel like you have some real skill, when in reality the house is just toying with you and decided to throw you a bone so you don't give up entirely and burn it to the ground. Then, when you get that first coat of paint on, you feel like you're really getting somewhere. Mike would use the roller, while I'd use the tiniest brush I could find to do the edge work.

"How can you stand to use such a tiny brush?" he asked. "That looks so frustrating."

"You have to use a tiny brush if you want to get it just right," I explained. "I like the tiny brush."

Mike loves the satisfaction of covering huge areas in a short period of time, while I find that the more tedious the work, the more I enjoy it. We are like this in other aspects of our lives as well. He's excellent at making big, sweeping decisions, while you'll find me spending four hours using Q-tips to clean the track of the sliding glass door. You can see why he's better at making money.

We were in the middle of transforming our dining room from the set of a 1960s Pall Mall commercial into something a little more twenty-first century when our dog, a chocolate Lab, came charging through the room with a toy in her mouth. She was in the middle of one of those psycho puppy runs when they run so fast that it seems their butts are tucked underneath their bodies. She was oblivious to any sort of obstacle in her path and barreled into an overhang of a drop cloth that had been covering the dining room table. The drop cloth somehow adhered to her as she kept moving. In slow motion horror, she galloped forward as the drop cloth transformed into a puppy cape. It slid from the table, and the open gallon of crimson paint that had been sitting on it came crashing and splashing to the floor. I reached forward, my hands open and fingers splayed, as if I might somehow catch the liquid, which was akin to trying take back the moment of having loudly passed gas in a crowded and otherwise silent room. It simply can't be done. A yellowed carpet that previously displayed only cigarette burns now held both cigarette burns and what appeared to be giant pools of blood. This might sound like a disaster, but I'd take a crime scene over the set of a Pall Mall commercial any day.

Our biggest success, perhaps because it required the least amount of skill, was clearing debris. I've always excelled at throwing things away. This applies to both trash and things that shouldn't be thrown away at all. I simply love to purge—only when it comes to physical things outside of my body, though, as this habit has never translated to an eating disorder.[19]

---

[19] *Contrary to any sort of eating disorder, I find that I'm exceptionally skilled when it comes to eating. For more information, refer to chapter 12: "How to Be Chubby."*

I'm not sure where my inclination to purge comes from, though I did move often as a child, sometimes once a year. This meant that packing up a lot of things was tiresome or what my mother would have described as "a royal pain in the ass." (Apparently, royalty experience ass pains on a far greater level than us common folk.)

As such, I learned not to accumulate clutter, because it meant more work later, when it was once again time to move. I adopted this to the extreme, and I consider throwing things away to be my chief hobby. I'd be excellent at clearing the home of a hoarder, but only if that person were already dead. If they were alive, they'd find my tactics too ruthless, and I'd probably make them cry. I don't want to make anyone cry, especially a hoarder. They have enough sorrow as it is, drowning in unopened packaging for As-Seen-On-TV products that they bought but will never use.

Our dilapidated home required clearing a lot of debris in and around the property (yay for me!). Both man-made items and layers of rotting leaves had accumulated over the years. This was fine, since I'm as good at throwing away nature as I am at disposing of tchotchkes. And truth be told, I like the smell of rotting leaves. They should mimic that scent for a line of perfumes, candles, and soaps. The company could be called Decay. I'd buy their stuff.

After many years and thousands of dollars, the home was finally habitable, so naturally it was time for us to move. We relocated to Idaho and purchased a home that had been inhabited by a hoarder. Luckily, she'd already died, so I didn't have to break her heart. She never had to watch as I coldly swept the detritus of her life into heavy-duty garbage bags.

The house was a plain brick structure with a low roof.

It had boring windows and a long set of decayed wicker blinds, inexplicably hung on the outside of the house. A thousand cigarette burns patterned the carpet, which was apparently the marker of homes to which we were attracted. The built-in cabinetry, circa 1950, had a sheen to it, almost like varnish until you moved closer and realized it was grease. Many of the cabinets were open, and you could tell that a relative had been in the process of sorting through the dead woman's belongings and then at some point simply gave up. The counter was home to piles of things, objects sorted into groups. One pile held what must have been two hundred pairs of scissors. A few were the standard size, but most were tiny, like the scissors from a travel-sized sewing kit, or appeared to be medical-grade scissors (I don't know if that's really a thing; I just made it up, but go with it) used to snip stitches. It seemed she'd collected them. As I boxed them up for the thrift store, I wondered where they'd end up in the world. Would the scissors stay together and become the property of another scissor hoarder? Or end up scattered across a variety of landfills? I'm fairly certain I'm the only one who wonders such things.

Overall, the house exuded death and decay and neglect.

It was perfect.

Not least of all because it necessitated renting a dumpster, one of my favorite pastimes. Whenever I rent a dumpster, I feel like I'm giving Mother Nature a tittie-twister. And who would do such a thing? I would, I guess.

A tittie-twister, if you're not in the know, is an abominable act that one person does to another. It is grabbing another person's nipple and then twisting it. This is extremely painful. Please don't try it at home. Or anywhere. Those big girls in junior high, the ones who got their periods before everyone else and fought viciously after school, they employed the tittie-twister in their schoolyard brawls. They also ripped hair from one another's scalps and clawed at eyes. Though I haven't seen it firsthand, I also imagine tittie-twisters to be common in boys' high school locker rooms. Not during brawls, of course, but amongst friends. Because some high school boys seem to show affection for one another by inflicting great pain. I don't know why they do this, but they do. When my husband sees buddies from high school, meetings that only occur every five or ten years, it's not uncommon for them to randomly tackle one another or attempt a headlock. A tittie-twister would not surprise me.

A dumpster means that I'm going to contribute to a landfill on a large scale. And for this reason, it feels like I'm giving Mother Nature a tittie-twister. *I'm sorry*, I want to say. *Can't you take this as a sign of affection? Like those boys who show their friendship through small acts of violence?*

I imagine Mother Nature answering: *No, bitch.*

My husband does not share my urge to purge. In fact, when he loses something, he immediately accuses me of "tidying" the missing object.

"Amanda, I can't find my keys."

"Did you leave them in the truck?"

"No," he'll insist. "I put them *right here* on the kitchen counter."

"Are you sure?"

"Yes, I came in, and I put them right here."

"I haven't seen them."

Then comes the accusation…

"Are you sure you didn't *tidy* them?"

What he's saying is that on one of my cleaning binges,

I've likely misplaced his keys. And yes, I clean, I move things around, but I've also learned over the years to tidy his things in the exact place where they reside, so nothing gets moved. Alternatively, I'll collect his flotsam and jetsam, put it in a pile on his side of the bed, thereby freeing the living room from a layer of Mike, and tell him that's where he should look if he's missing anything.

"Yes, I am sure I did not *tidy* your keys." At that point, I'll walk to his truck, retrieve his keys, and give him the I-told-you-so look I have perfected these past two decades.

Though he's neither a purger nor a hoarder, Mike has mad dumpster skills, which I never knew were a thing until we rented our first dumpster together. It was sort of like buying our first bed together, only different. I assumed that when it came to dumpsters, you just began chucking things in there. Not so. Mike will climb into the dumpster, despite numerous warnings on said dumpster not to do so, and arrange gutted couch cushions, broken chairs, and rusted gutters as if these were pieces of an intricate puzzle. When one is paying for a dumpster, one strives for maximum use of space. Not a square inch is to go to waste. If yard debris is involved, he'll jump up and down on it to compact leaves and brush, or possibly attack it with a sledgehammer. Watching my husband climb inside a dumpster to make sure we get as much room as possible to throw things away, well, honestly, he's never been hotter.

It's been a while now since we've bought a hoarder home. Our deck isn't a death trap. We're no longer likely to find a hidden cupboard filled with baby doll limbs. (That's not something that's ever happened to me, but it could, dammit.) And our appliances will not benefit from a can of spray paint. But I still dream about our next dumpster rental.

There's always something to "tidy."

At our current home, we (meaning Mike) repurposed a few old pallets and turned them into two composting bays. Now, instead of disposing of nature, I can turn it back into nature. The feel-good element cannot be overstated. I no longer feel like I'm giving Mother Nature a tittie-twister. Now it's more like I'm brushing her hair after using copious amounts of detangler, so it doesn't hurt at all, not one little bit.

This isn't to say that I don't have needless items in my possession. My garage is home to a gigantic bin of "artwork" that my children have produced over the years. This is likely to include a crude circle with the caption "Hny Nut Chrrrrio," but I'll be damned if I can bring myself to throw those gems away.

When my father died, I asked my sister to send me something from his office. The care package I received included a stapler circa 1972 and a letter opener, which I'm pretty sure I gave him when I was a kid. I went through a phase of wanting to give gifts to people, and I saved up my money to do so. For one of my scheduled weekend visits at my father's house, my mother dropped me off along with a Santa-worthy sack of wrapped gifts, one each for my father, stepmother, stepsister, and stepbrother. This could have been a ploy to be liked more or feel accepted, and I'm sure it just came across as trying too hard. My gift-giving stage eventually faded, and I started stealing things instead. I found it to be more rewarding.

My father's letter opener now resides in my closet, not for the purpose of opening letters but because I envision myself someday stabbing a would-be intruder in the neck with it.[20]

————

[20] *It could happen.*

My purging tendencies are not great for the earth but are a boon to the consumer economy. For instance, every few years, I'm convinced I need a denim jacket. I'll see an ad picturing a woman half my size doing something ridiculous like skateboarding in a flowy skirt while a bulldog trots happily beside her on a leash. The more contrived the picture, the more I'm in. Sold. The advertising machine works on me, because I'll carry this image in my subconscious. I'll want the carefree, naturally blissful feel of the model in the photo for myself. I'm not going to take up skateboarding, because I would kill myself, and I'm not going to get a bulldog, because my husband has no tolerance for any canine other than a Labrador, so I begin to attribute all of the things I want as stemming from the denim jacket. I'll adopt my typical mode of shopping, which means I'll try something on, and though it won't quite fit, won't look like I want it to, and won't be quite what I'm after, I'll buy it anyway, convinced that it will be perfect by the end of next week, because maybe by then I'll have shed an extra pound or twenty-five. It could happen. But it never does, so over time, the jacket collects dust in my closet until I find myself in another cycle of purging. I'll free myself from the denim jacket and all its broken promises, only until the next time I come across an ad promoting a life that is not my own. This time, the woman might be walking along a beach at sunrise, or some other similar activity in which I never partake. Instead of the skateboard and bulldog, she'll be wearing a large, floppy hat that somehow looks bohemian chic on her and another article of clothing I could never pull off, like white linen pants. And for some reason, this image, though just as unlikely as the first one, will implant itself into my brain and fester there, until I'm once again compelled to spend forty-five to seventy-five dollars on an ill-fitting denim jacket that will gather dust in my closet until the cycle repeats itself.

Whenever I come into contact with someone's hoarding tendencies, I experience a mixture of fascination and revulsion. Inevitably, I want to know more. Did the hoarding start slowly and increase over time? Or was it there from the start, beginning with the compilation of a secret stash of pacifiers in the crib? Was it trauma induced? Passed down from a previous generation? So many questions. There are plenty of "normal" people who have secret hoarding tendencies, which is why you might have friends over for dinner and then never receive a reciprocal invitation. Perhaps you let this eat away at you, wondering why they don't like you, if you offended them, or if they found your cooking to be atrocious. You could need therapy to work through the perceived slight, when in reality they just don't want you to see their collection of eight years' worth of newspapers or the room they keep full of empty cardboard egg cartons.

When my mother visits a lifelong friend of hers from high school, she'll text me pictures from various rooms in his house.

Here's a picture of a collection of broken lamps…

This is a tower consisting of eight toasters, all new and unopened, still in the box…

Here's half an avocado he refuses to throw away, insisting it's still good even though it's black. He keeps it in the kitchen cabinet, not the fridge…

Check out Wayne's ketchup bottle. The contents are dark brown like barbecue sauce and expired in 1998…

Most disturbing to me, of all of these instances, is the half of an avocado. Hoarding things that have the potential to rot is taking hoarding to a previously unfathomable level. Wayne is a smart guy. Why, then, would he keep a perishable item in his cabinet and respond as he did to my mother, with both shock and disdain when she suggested throwing it away? Does he think that avocados can be aged? Like cheese? And the bigger question, did he ever actually eat it? Did it make him sick? Or is it still sitting in that cabinet, turning into avocado jerky? And if so, is there a market for such a product?

The fact that my mother continues to visit Wayne, and stay in his house of horrors when she does so, is not so much a testament to their friendship as it is evidence that my mother has the same morbid fascination[21] with hoarding that I do.

Wayne is also living proof that hoarding is not a class issue. Hoarding is not a symptom of poverty-stricken folks who can't let go. Wayne has money and means and time.

He also has eleven broken televisions.

Though I'm fairly certain I'm not in danger of going down the hoarder path, I also recognize that many of my tendencies have the potential of becoming just as disruptive. I clean and I plan, which might sound like positive attributes, but sometimes I fantasize about taking these things too far. For example, I can clean my bathroom and as I'm doing so, note the fact that condensation has formed tiny marks on the ceiling, and that if I just get out a stepladder and some cleaning supplies, I can probably eliminate said marks. While I'm up there, I may realize that the light fixture could benefit from

---

21 *My mother's morbid fascinations extend well beyond hoarding and include all aspects of true crime, not limited to murder and abuse, though those are hot topics. She could probably relate the life stories of Jeffrey Dahmer, Ted Bundy, BTK, and Aileen Wuornos (one of her favorites) in fairly accurate detail. If such a thing as serial killer* Jeopardy *existed, my mom would rock it.*

being dismantled and cleaned, piece by piece. If I don't take these actions, it is all I will think about. If I do, I'll disappear into the bathroom for three days, during which time my kitchen will have fallen into a state of unhygienic disarray. And the cycle continues.

When I worked in an office building, I used to set out my outfits the night before, so that early morning decision-making could be eliminated. I'd wake, shower, and have my office attire laid out and ready to go. Then I realized I could gain even more ground on this particular hamster wheel by preselecting my outfits for the entire week, at which point I'd removed all of the clothes from closet, creating a maelstrom of fabric which threatened to overtake the bedroom.

Similarly, I could pack my lunch the night before. Or I could pack *many* lunches, thereby again getting even further ahead on the hamster wheel. Unfortunately, food goes bad. And before I knew it, not only was my bedroom impassable, but my fridge was filled with inedible sandwiches, including the occasional long-departed avocado. As it turns out, Wayne and I aren't so different after all.

CHAPTER 7
THE BIG SUCK

When Mike and I were first married, the internet was in its infancy. If you were looking for a job back then, you bought a newspaper and perused the want ads. It was quaintly analog, like my insistence on using a paper calendar and crossing off my to-do list with a good old-fashioned pencil.

I'm not sure exactly what this particular ad said, but it spoke to me. It probably flattered the reader, said that if you had what it took, there would be no limit to your potential. It must also have stipulated no experience necessary, because though I had a varied background by then, I had no sales experience.

I did have clown experience. I'd worked as Bingo the Clown at a chain restaurant in the mall. Actually, I was one of three Bingos, one of my fellow Bingos being my best friend. At the hiring fair, the manager said he thought of me more in the hostess role, but I fought for Bingo. I wanted to be different. I didn't want to be one of a dozen hostesses. I wanted to be one of three clowns.

Bingo was a fairly cushy gig. When I first arrived at work, I could spend the better part of an hour putting on my makeup, wig, and costume. My friend and I would often take breaks, which meant we'd sneak into the employee bathroom and smoke cigarettes, to the dismay of half the waitresses. (The other half also snuck into the bathroom and smoked cigarettes.) In hindsight, I can imagine few dining scenarios worse than having a nicotine-reeking clown approach my child at a restaurant. Eventually, Bingo was phased out. I don't like to think that I was the death of this character, but it's possible.

The alluring ad in the paper was vague. It spoke of sales, but sales with tact. It sounded classy somehow. I imagined myself owning pantsuits and a briefcase. Maybe even a pager, because just as it was the age of finding employment by perusing want ads in the newspaper, it was also the era of pagers. Super high-tech people got paged. Then they searched out a pay phone. Picturing myself with a pantsuit, briefcase, and pager was similar to the image I had of myself when I dreamed of working as a spy, but requiring less brainpower and with more physical safety.

I called the number from the ad and after a brief chat was told I'd been accepted for an early interview. Obviously, the person on the other end of the line could sense my innate abilities just from hearing my voice. I was special. They knew it, and I knew it.

Apparently, there were lots of special people, because a group of twelve of us showed up at the interview, which was suddenly referred to as "training," which we all took to mean that we'd successfully passed the interview stage without even knowing it. *Yay, us!* Training took place in a nondescript room of an equally bland building. No signage existed. Not a single clue to hint at the entity's name or purpose. After two full days, we were excited about our earning potential but still had no idea what we'd be selling.

This period of ignorance was the perfect time for me to live out fantasies in my head. Maybe this was the first step in me becoming a spy after all! That was surely why there'd been so much secrecy surrounding this whole endeavor. Their want ad had likely been crafted with language designed to appeal to people with the right personality for espionage-type work. I wondered if I'd get a holster to carry a sleek, ladylike gun. Maybe even two. One for my hip and then a discreet backup gun hidden on my upper thigh. I was going to be dangerous and sexy and well compensated.

At the end of the second day, we were shown a video that revealed for whom we were working. The fact that two days of training had passed and we still had no idea what we were being trained for should have been a red flag. And how they even managed such a feat was downright artful, a classic bait and switch. When the video ended, we looked around at one another, slightly stunned and trying to keep ourselves on the high of all that earning potential. We'd be selling vacuum cleaners. Door to door.

Was there a bright side? It wasn't mucking out portable toilets. It wasn't working in a slaughterhouse.[22]

"I'm out. I'm sorry. This is not my thing," said a middle-aged man. He was trim with long white hair. We'd come to know him as the musician. Music is a tough business, and he'd been looking for something to pay the bills. Once he left, the trainer made a few digs at him, parroting the "not my thing" phrase and reminding us that the man had just declared earning money to be not his thing. Those who remained, he assured us, were the smart ones.

With the cat out of the bag, or the multipiece vacuum cleaner out of its case, training turned to how to use the equipment. It was a heavy, complicated, clunky contraption,

_____

22 *That's all I could come up with.*

but the sucking power was truly something. We learned how to demonstrate the phenomenal suction, first by using a regular vacuum and then going over the same spot with our superior product to show just how much more dirt we could retrieve from the lucky carpet square.

Two of us were singled out in the group as potential rising stars—me and a handsome young man.[23] I suppose the two of us were just the most normal, and the rest were hopeless. The more I looked around, the less special we looked. There was an old man who wore incredibly bulky adult diapers that bulged from his tight polyester pants. He broke my heart. Not because of his age and frailty and need for the thickest adult diapers one could buy, but because in addition to all that, he was desperate for work and hoped that he might make some money selling vacuum cleaners. Others had physical, social, or mental defects, it was clear. But the baby-faced man and me, we signified potential. The managers wanted to see us soar. We would be the next generation of rainmakers.

I was quickly paired up with the chief rainmaker. She was a single mom and the best closer there was. When she walked into the training room to introduce herself and tell us the story of how vacuum cleaners had turned her depressing and financially woeful existence into a life full of joy and money, they played "I'm Every Woman." She dazzled us with her exuberance. She was likable, relatable, and lived and breathed vacuums.[24] The message was clear. I was to be the next version of her.

Cheryl took me under her wing and to her next

---

23 *Think John Legend but a foot taller.*

24 **Cough*Hack*Choke**

appointment to demonstrate the vacuum at a home. The nice young couple seemed interested in the added sucking power of our model, and Cheryl peppered them with facts of all the things they were currently breathing in,[25] from which *our* vacuum could save them. At one point, she went out to her car to retrieve something and told me that I could go ahead and demonstrate how they could use the vacuum to clean the curtains. When she left the room, I held a vacuum extension up to one of their curtains and said something feeble along the lines of, "You just go like this." I turned the vacuum on, and it was immediately apparent that I was going to rip the curtains from the wall. I turned it off. "Um, maybe we'll just wait for Cheryl to get back."

"Did you show them how to clean the curtains?" she asked upon her return with her dazzling, bleached smile.

"Well, it seemed like it might be too strong…"

Cheryl laughed it off, reduced the suction power, and demonstrated flawless curtain sucking. I hadn't known that reducing the suction power was an option. Apparently, I'd zoned out during that part of training. I was worried that I might have cost her the sale, but she did that on her own.

Everyone was pleasant until Cheryl went in for the kill. After the demonstration, she put a hard sell on the couple. She was brutal. Ruthless. And rude.

"I don't like this. Why do you people do this?" the wife pleaded.

"Do what?" Cheryl asked.

"You're pressuring me with these sales tactics!"

"I'm not pressuring. Who's pressuring?" Cheryl countered,

---

25 *Cough*Hack*Choke*

holding up her hands defensively.

The husband sat mute and worthless by his wife as she neared tears. Years later, I would learn the term *gaslighting* and instantly remember Cheryl acting as if she hadn't been pressuring the couple into purchasing a two-thousand-dollar vacuum.

On the drive back to the office, Cheryl chatted. "Can you believe that woman?" she asked. "Why did she get so upset? I wasn't pressuring anyone. Geez."

I nodded, simply because I was in her car and therefore felt obligated to agree with her. *Is that what she has to tell herself?* I wondered. *Does she continue the denial even after she's gone, because then she won't have to face the awful truth of her behavior?* And I knew then that if I was going to be a rising star, if I was going to make money selling vacuum cleaners, I would have to turn into Cheryl. I would have to be bullish and bring housewives to tears and make them fear the dust mites in their homes. This, I could not do.

Management was clearly disappointed that I didn't want to become the next Cheryl. But they also weren't ready to let me go. I was transitioned into a new role: knocker. "It's easy," they said. All I would have to do was knock on doors and make the offer. If they'd let us demonstrate our vacuum, we'd deep clean a carpet or piece of furniture for free. I was the one trying to get the appointment, so the Cheryls and John Legends could swoop in later and sell the two-thousand-dollar vacuum. I could do that, I thought. How hard could it be?

It turns out that knocking on doors is terribly difficult. Especially when you're already afraid of people, and particularly afraid of other people being mean to you. There are many who have mastered this. They remain detached, like a bad retina. When someone slammed a door in *my* face, however, I wanted to sit down and cry right there. Straight from my fully attached retinas.

Years later, someone knocked on my door with an offer to clean a piece of my furniture if I'd let her demonstrate her vacuum. I was determined to be nice to her, because I felt for her. I politely told her that I wasn't interested.

"We can deep clean a carpet or sofa," she continued.

"No, really, I'm not interested. There's no sale here."

"It doesn't cost anything and just takes about fifteen minutes."

She kept ignoring me and forging forth.[26]

"You know, I had your job," I confided. "I used to be a knocker. I know how it works."

She didn't bat an eye and kept extolling the virtues of her product. She grew belligerent and rude, and I realized why so many people had slammed doors in my face. They were anticipating *this* scenario and trying to cut me off before I got that far. But I *never* got that far. I lasted two days as a door knocker before my fragile ego could no longer deal with learning that I was hated by strangers.

Though I might deny it if asked to my face, inherently I want people to like me. This is at odds with the fact that I often, inexplicably, do unlikable things, like try to sell vacuum cleaners.

Rather than bemoan these and other failures, I like to focus on the benefits. Surely, I grew during that time. It must have been a character-building experience.[27] Self-helpers love to talk about the importance of getting out of your comfort zone.

---

26 *She was a better knocker than I ever was.*

27 *My mother always describes shitty situations as "character-building."*

If they're right, then I'm amazing. Because I'm uncomfortable more often than not. Selling vacuum cleaners was about as far out of my comfort zone as me running for political office or attending church or doing one of those polar plunges or pretending to know what eyebrow threading is.[28]

Eventually, I came to terms with the fact that while it's healthy to get out of your comfort zone, that doesn't necessarily mean that what you do on a day-to-day basis, how you make your living, should be outside of your comfort zone. It also took me many decades to realize that I don't need to say yes to every job opportunity that comes along. Somehow, I grew up feeling that compulsion, that if you were presented with a job, you were lucky and should be grateful and do the job, even if that meant shoveling shit, literally (which I've done) and metaphorically (which I've done). Everyone should have to do some sort of manure relocation at some point, for the character-building aspect, but when all is said and done, it's worth it to seek out employment that resides squarely within your comfort zone, because you're likely to be good at it and have less chance of ending up hating your life.

As I see it, the problem is that too often we think, *Okay, I'm most comfortable when eating carbs, sleeping, and offering my unsolicited opinion.*

As far as I know, that's not yet a combination that leads to gainful employment, unless you're a movie critic, and I have no idea how to get that job.

Then there's the sad fact that most of the time, when you're *really* looking for a job, it's because you really *need* a job. As in, I have two days before the electricity is shut off. Or,

---

28 *I still don't know what eyebrow threading is.*

I could pay this month's rent if I sell my car, but then I won't be able to get to the job I don't yet have to pay next month's rent. Having the emotional room to consider what is and is not in our comfort zone doesn't usually coincide with the times in our lives when we're desperate for employment.

In addition to building character, my vacuum cleaner sales experience taught me that door-to-door sales was well outside my comfort zone, but vacuuming was not. I'd simply been approaching it from the wrong angle. For many years, I ended up cleaning other people's houses, sometimes part-time for supplemental income, and at other times as a full-time gig. While others might balk at the idea of cleaning up someone else's crap, I felt quite at home in it. I would guess that the mature point of view to take when being permitted into someone else's home is not to judge—to be respectful and impartial about the state of their home and its contents. That approach is, in my opinion, a missed opportunity and a complete waste of time. Especially when you are left alone in someone else's home, you have the opportunity to judge without having to disguise your judgment. To make assumptions about the people who live there and develop story lines in your head about why they are the way they are and, by comparison, how much better your own life is.[29]

During my time as a cleaner, I was exposed to a fascinating mix of American families. At one point I cleaned the homes of two women, unknown to each other, who were both dying of cancer. In the first, I'd been hired by the woman's friends who wanted to help, though the friend who hired me confided that

---

[29] *To all my former cleaning clients: just kidding, I would never think along those lines.*

the dying woman was actually kind of a bitch. I found this to be true.

The other woman dying of cancer was gracious and kind and all the things that good humans should strive to be. The heartbreak of her situation was compounded by a living room littered with books designed to guide small children through the death of a parent.

Then there was the idyllic home, what seemed the nesting ground of a picture-perfect family. In the middle of the dining room table sat a wooden caddy that held place mats and cutlery for four, and I could picture the daughters taking turns setting the table. They divorced soon after I was hired, which was a bonus for me, as both parties kept me on, so the one job turned into two.

I cleaned the home of a young Mormon couple with a new baby. The woman asked me to do the kitchen first, as her bible study group would be coming over soon. A dozen other young mothers arrived. I didn't hear any talk of the bible though, as their meeting focused more on an upcoming trip to Salt Lake City so that they could shop at IKEA. Inexplicably, the home was filled with items that still had price tags hanging off of them, everything from wall art to bedside lamps to shelving units. Perhaps those items were later returned to IKEA.

A much older family lived at another Mormon home I cleaned. Two adults, three teenagers, each of them hunkered down in separate bedrooms in front of separate televisions, seemingly as far from one another as possible. The house was filthy, the air hostile, no matter how many pictures of Jesus adorned the walls.

I've cleaned the homes of lesbians who always tried to feed me soup, elderly gay millionaires who kept a thousand-square-foot room filled with porcelain dolls, and hunters whose living rooms were filled with animal heads and lamps made out of dead birds. I once cleaned a home so immaculate that I'm pretty sure it was cleaner before I started than after I finished. At that particular home, I also knocked down a garland of decorative faux greenery, proving my suspicion that my presence did more harm than good.

Cleaning someone else's home is downright enjoyable when they're not there, when you can listen to music, belt it out, judge away, and marvel at what a fantastic job you've done (except for the occasion when you knock down the faux greenery) and how you're obviously underpaid. The worst, however, is when you have someone standing there looking over your shoulder, telling you that you missed a spot, and you have to muster up every cell of discipline in your being to keep sarcasm out of your voice when you respond.[30] If you're cleaning homes, that's often the trickiest part.

If you're on the other side of the equation, if you're the one having your home cleaned, consider throwing away the detritus of your sex life before the cleaner arrives. I once cleaned a home where the couple, who were young and hip and had an apparently healthy sex life, left KY Jelly and sex tissues on the bed. I did what most people would do: I pulled the comforter up to hide the evidence, because that's what I hope a housecleaner would do if confronted with tissues and lube in my bedroom. Perhaps each of them assumed the

---

[30] *Some people think that teenagers are disrespectful because of their overuse of sarcasm and eye rolls, but I think we all still have a bit of that in us; we've simply been forced to play nice and work in the real world, so we've learned how to mask such reactions.*

other one had pulled up the comforter. I'm fairly sure neither of them realized they'd left these little gems out for me to see. I believe this to be the case, because there was no sign of discomfort from them when I showed up the following week. In fact, they seemed more comfortable with me than ever.

"Hey, Amanda," said the wife, who looked effortlessly cool and worldly and confident. "Do you know where we might score some pot?"

Incidentally, I did not know. *No one has ever asked me that before*, I thought, *because most people who know me also know that I'm probably not a good source for such information. But I should say something*. My mind raced. *And I can't just say no, because that will make her uncomfortable and she'll realize I'm not the person to ask and maybe she'll freak out and think I'm a narc!* Only now in looking back do I see how much effort I put into making her feel comfortable about all of the things she was already comfortable with, including her sexual accessories[31] and recreational drug use. And in the moment of realizing I had been mistaken for someone who might know where a person could score some pot, I came up with a feeble answer.

"Um, maybe you should go down to the pizza place," I suggested, "and ask someone there." The words didn't seem idiotic as they were coming out of my mouth, but then stagnated in the air between us.

Should I say more? Give more details to add some false credibility to my story? What pizza place? There are a million pizza places in Boise. And who would one ask? Maybe a guy named Lou! That seemed plausible for some reason, despite the fact that the only creature named Lou I knew was my sister's

---

31 *Sexessories?*

female cat. She saved me from uttering any further inanities.

"It's cool," she said. "Just thought I'd ask."

And I realized then the answer to so many questions.

Do you know where to score some pot?

Do you want to sell vacuums door to door?

Do you consider yourself a people person?

Do you know what eyebrow threading is?

It's shockingly simple but always a struggle: the answer is just to say "no."

CHAPTER 8
MY CORPORATE LADDER BROKE

Eventually, I returned to the want ads. I needed to aim higher than door-to-door vacuum sales. And I would no longer be fooled by the vague-but-enticing language in the ads that *led* to vacuum cleaner sales. I learned to spot them, peppered throughout the paper like fool's gold. After all, I had a degree. Surely, I could put it to use. I could be a professional.

At the time, we lived in a suburb of San Francisco. I imagined myself reading every day while letting the ferry deliver me to the city, where I'd take the subway to some sort of district. Like the Financial District, not the red-light district. Something classy. There, I'd have an office and do important things alongside important people. Eventually, their importance might rub off on me.

I wore a modest skirt into the city for my first interview and soon realized that the streets of San Francisco are inexplicably windy. I walked not with confidence and the air of a professional, or even a would-be professional, but hunched over and pinning down my clothes, lest my skirt fly up over my head, both exposing me and blinding me, at which point I'd stumble into traffic and die.

My first interview was at a law office in need of administrative support. The lawyer was a kind-looking, middle-aged man in a lawyerly suit and large, dated glasses that reminded me of the square frames I'd worn as a child. It went well, or at least I thought it did at the time. Only after I left did it occur to me that when he asked about my SAT scores, and I proudly told him how I fared (above average, but below astonishing), he'd actually been talking about the LSAT. Because if I was applying at a law firm, even in an administrative support position, surely I'd taken the LSAT and was on track to become a lawyer. I had no intention of doing either. He didn't call me back.

Another interview I had really *was* in the Financial District and was more in line with my experience. I was unclear on the exact specifications of the job, but it had to do with banking and Russians. Maybe it was a money-laundering operation. I can't be sure, but I *was* sure that the interviewer very much wanted to hire me. There weren't many job seekers with degrees in Russian at the time. As opposed to being an asset, though, the language intimidated me. I'd forgotten much of the Russian I knew in my youth, and I had nothing resembling a Russian vocabulary of financial lingo. I didn't fully understand the meanings of "debit" and "credit" in English, much less in Russian. As well, the job entailed speaking with Russians about financial dealings (perhaps legal, perhaps not) over the phone. Anyone struggling in a second language knows how terrifying the phone can be. In person, you can supplement with facial expressions and sign language and, if need be, stick figures drawn on scraps of paper to get your point across. Talking on the phone takes all of those fallback tools away. Even now, when we find ourselves in a different country and I am tasked with making a phone call and communicating in another language, I begin to sweat. A forty-five-second conversation will leave me looking as if I've just completed an

Ironman competition. Maybe that's not true, because if I'd just completed an Ironman competition, there's a good possibility that I'd be dead. And when I'm forced to speak on the phone in another language, I don't look dead, just very sweaty.

My interviewer called me twice after our meeting, wanting to know if I'd like to discuss future employment. But honestly, banking with Russians sounded just about as painful as door-to-door vacuum sales.

I ended up working as a waitress, not far from our home, at a restaurant I won't name. I *will* divulge the nickname I used for it, which is Crapplebee's. During my Crapplebee's interview, no one asked me about my fluency in other languages or what I'd scored on a standardized test. The questions centered more on whether or not I had a working vehicle and if I had any prior drug convictions or outstanding felonies. I turned out to be an ideal candidate.

Crapplebee's was neither a great nor terrible job. There was the kind manager who would smoke cigarettes with us in the storeroom, the mean manager who would smoke cigarettes with us in the storeroom and also seemed as if he might be doing massive amounts of cocaine, and the female manager everyone hated, because she was the female manager. Others would come and go over time. Ramon, the cheerful waiter, was promoted to manager, and I later learned he ran a scheme with one of my fellow waitresses. Whenever she had a customer pay in cash, she'd tell Ramon, and he'd comp the entrees on the bill, as if the customer had complained and he was making it right. Then he and the waitress would split the cash. That same waitress later had an affair with Wade, the young manager who transferred in from another location, perhaps because he'd been bonking the employees there as well.

My Crapplebee's customers were a crapshoot. Some were okay. Others would sneak out without paying or be rude because they could, and maybe that was the highlight of their little lives. I soon wormed my way onto the expo line, which I enjoyed because it meant less contact with people. An expo is the middleman between the cooks and the waitstaff. The expo line was also like putting together an endless line of little puzzles, and I like puzzles. I matched food to orders, adding ramekins of ketchup and kale garnishes when necessary. It's worth noting that during this time, no one knew that kale was edible. It was only used for garnish. No one bought a bag of kale at the grocery store and thought to work it into a salad of some sort or cook it or blend it. I'm not even sure we knew it was an actual plant, and maybe thought it was synthetic greenery. No one dared sample it.

I was good at the expo line, and if I ever had to return to the restaurant industry, that's what I would do. It meant protecting cooks from waiters and vice versa. Keeping the peace but still not having to deal with the customers. I also liked busing tables. I'm good at cleaning things, and again, it saved me from having to make nice with the customers.

I worked a few other jobs over the following years, from accounting to bartending to behind-the-scenes crew in movies and television.[32] That may sound glamorous, and parts of it were, but for the most part it was work in a setting where massive egos collided daily, mine among them.

As far as the corporate world, I was fairly certain it wasn't for me. I didn't seem to fit in there, mostly because no matter

---

[32] *See chapter 9: "Thunda Chicken Blong Jesus Christ."*

how hard I tried, I just couldn't care. For a while, I processed payroll at a company that did building maintenance. The highlight of the day was deciding from where we'd order food for lunch, and my pant size grew considerably during my time there. Most of my work was in coding antiquated payroll sheets for maintenance workers, with incomprehensible discrepancies between the rates paid to union and nonunion workers. I thought about Jimmy Hoffa often.

Years would pass before I'd begin writing full-time. I didn't get to that point because my writing eventually made enough money for me to do it full-time, but because my *husband* eventually made enough money for me to do it full-time. It can't be easy being married to a constant financial strain, but he never complains about it. In any case, there's no getting away from it; writing is in my blood.

My father was a writer, though he was the type of writer who made money, sometimes very good money, writing books. He wrote countless articles in his early career and a few dozen books after that, including *Midnight Express* with Billy Hayes and *Not Without My Daughter* with Betty Mahmoody. When people had a story to tell, but maybe not the writing chops to go with it, he excelled at helping them turn their stories into books, sometimes bestsellers and movies to boot. He also wrote books on his own or with his wife. He was a craftsman with words, not only in print but also spoken. For example, no one could deliver a eulogy like my dad; he'd have everyone laughing and crying and wondering when his next funeral appearance would be, because he was so damn entertaining.

My father was not the type of parent to ever *let* someone win at something, because if you couldn't beat him, you certainly didn't deserve to win. This went from childhood, when he'd obliterate me in chess matches, likely with the secret hope that I'd emerge as a child prodigy and the growing realization that that was never going to happen, through to adulthood when we played Words with Friends for the last few years of his life. When we first started playing, he offered rare praise, letting me know that while he never lost a game, of all the people with whom he played, I was the only one who came close to beating him. Over time, our matches got closer. Then I'd occasionally win and walk around on a temporary high at having beaten my unbeatable father. When I started winning regularly, and then winning more than I lost, I silently gloated at how smart I'd become. My brain cells were obviously growing stronger. But alas, my increase in wins against my father were not what they seemed. I wasn't experiencing a boost in brainpower; he was declining. One day, he simply stopped playing altogether. Three years later, he died. Though I don't know the official cause on his death certificate, the true culprit was dementia. While it was horrific to see what happened to both his mind and body, it was also a strangely appropriate way of him asserting his final win, because only a brain-obliterating disease could throw him off his game. Well done, Dad.

Games with my mother were always far more enjoyable, not simply because I would win without her letting me, but also because they were filled with more laughter than lessons. We used to play card games that required speed. My mother has many wonderful qualities—for instance, she can clean the track of a sliding glass door like nobody's business (it is from her that I inherited that particular skill)—but speed is not one of them. Nonetheless, she played hand after hand with me of a card game that she knew she was only ever destined to lose, because it was fun. Because the two of us would laugh until reduced to fits of tears about how badly I'd beat her, time and time again.

These may not seem like great lessons that prepared me for the corporate world or the real world, but in reality, they were equally valuable. Winning against my mother was just as constructive as losing to my father. Because regardless of whether you win or lose, a situation can be any combination of unbearable, pointless, and aggravating if you don't know how to navigate it with a sense of humor.

* * *

Mike and I had two daughters of our own. Emilia came first; Ivy followed two years later. When they were young, we encouraged entrepreneurship with the typical summer rites of passage like lemonade stands. This idea was always marred by the fact that my daughters would try to add other things for sale, like "art" or old hair clips. As far as the "art," I believe the quotation marks speak for themselves, and I can think of few items I want to spend money on less than a child's used hair accessories. Then they'd add old stuffed animals or kitchen utensils, which I'd never agreed they could sell, until what started as a lemonade stand ended up looking like a yard sale organized by elementary schoolers, which is exactly what it was.

In his effort to cultivate entrepreneurship (Mike is a serial entrepreneur, which is way better than a serial killer), Mike helped them set up a free coffee and hot chocolate stand on a busy street corner downtown. The beverages were free but handed to you by an endearing little girl with a large tip jar sitting nearby. Those kids made bank. Occasionally, a driver waiting at the stoplight would roll down his window and say, "Hey, kid, I don't need a coffee, but here's a twenty. Keep up the good work."

The entrepreneurial fire grew. Before long, we were talking about more serious business ideas. I voted for making candles or soap, because I've secretly always wanted to make candles and soap.[33] Instead, we ended up purchasing a cotton candy machine. We were on a trip in Thailand and saw a cotton candy vendor, which first planted the seed of the idea. We bought the girls each a bag of cotton candy that day, and though I pointed out the fact that the cotton candy vendor, who ate as much cotton candy as he sold, was missing most of his teeth, the idea still stuck. Mike was always concerned about how much sugar our daughters were capable of consuming, so I thought that might deter him, but the markup was too good. As a businessman, Mike was enchanted by the incredible return on investment. There is quite a gap between the cost of cotton candy mix and the price for which you can sell cotton candy.

Once back in the States, we filed the necessary business permits, designed a logo, and had T-shirts made. The Sugar Sisters were official and open for business. Incidentally, when we designed the Sugar Sisters' online presence, we learned that "Sugar Sisters" can have an entirely different meaning

---

[33] *I love burning candles and washing my body. I'm a hippie, but at least I'm not a dirty hippie, because of all the soap I use. I'm a crafty hippie and a wannabe homesteader, but my inclinations to honor this truth within me are constantly thwarted by family and other pesky things like logic and reality.*

and target audience.[34]

Of course, in addition to a cotton candy machine, you have to buy all of the accessories that go with it. This includes cotton candy mix, which is basically very fine, artificially colored and flavored sugar that you pour into the machine, which is then magically transformed into cotton candy. I'm sure there's science behind it, but for the sake of simplicity, let's just go with magic.

"What if we made organic cotton candy?" Mike suggested. "I mean, we can do regular cotton candy, but we could also come up with our own flavors and use organic sugar and freeze-dried fruits."

"That's an excellent idea," I agreed. "People love organic shit." And by shit, I meant any item other than actual shit. So, in addition to the cardboard cartons of cotton candy mix, Mike ordered a fifty-pound bag of organic sugar and bought bags of organic, freeze-dried fruits from Trader Joe's. It seemed

---

34 *Much like the time I tried to revisit a writing website I'd stumbled upon and enjoyed. I couldn't remember the name of it but knew it was something to do with black ink on white paper. When trying to find a website that deals with writing, do not, under any circumstances, type in a Google search for "black on white," especially if you are in a workplace setting, as I happened to be at the time. I don't care what other keywords you have to go along with it. Unless you are specifically seeking out interracial pornographic content, you will see a variety of images for which you are likely unprepared. As well, this particular instance occurred on a desktop computer. There was no laptop screen that could be quickly and easily shut, just a lot of fumbling about with a mouse and a mousepad to try to close that particular browser. Any apprehension I had about being discovered looking at a writers' website while at work evaporated. Because now I was just a pervert on company time.*

simple enough. We'd just put some of the fruit in the coffee grinder until it resembled a fine powder, then mix it with the organic sugar and throw it in the cotton candy machine. How hard could it be?

It's pretty hard. We managed to damage the machine right off the bat.

"Hmm," I said as the machine began to smoke and sputter, while the girls protested behind us, wondering when it would be their turn. They were, after all, the Sugar Sisters. "Perhaps we should start with the traditional cotton candy mix first and perfect that process before we start branching off into organic varieties."

"Good idea," Mike agreed.

We cleaned up the machine as best we could and started over. We were more confident on the second go-round, as by then we'd watched countless YouTube videos of people making cotton candy. We watched as one man demonstrated how easy it was. He made it right in his kitchen, as simple as if he were buttering toast.[35]

Our operation took place in our living room, and this time, with cotton candy mix, the machine worked spectacularly well. What we hadn't anticipated, however, was that strands of cotton candy would form quickly and fruitfully and fly through the air like migrating spiders, landing on everything in our home.

As the air became choked with sugar and difficult to breathe, Mike said, "I don't remember anything like this happening in that YouTube video."

At one point, it's possible that I yelled, "Shut it off!

––––––

[35] *I could mess this up if I really tried.*

Shut it off! Cut the power *now!*" as if I needed to disarm a nuclear reactor capable of destroying the planet. Because this is how I feel at the prospect of every surface and item in my home being covered with sugar.

After that, we moved the cotton candy machine onto the back deck, and later, in the winter months, into the garage. With practice, we got to a point where the girls were doing most of the work. Mike would fuss with the dials on the machine, and I would bag the spun sugar, but Emilia and Ivy were the ones who would bring it to life and roll it onto the large paper cones.

When we were able to successfully produce, package, and seal a few dozen bags of cotton candy, we took our freshly paid-for seller's permit and headed downtown. The differing sales approaches of our daughters were remarkable. Ivy would timidly ask strangers from afar, "Would you like to buy some cotton candy?" They never answered because I'm pretty sure no one heard her.

By contrast, Emilia approached people as if she might mug them.

"You wanna buy some cotton candy?" she'd demand, getting in their faces and blocking their paths. *"Do you? Do you?"*

Most people were frightened and sidestepped her in a mix of alarm and confusion. It wasn't the typical behavior of a ten-year-old girl. Mike and I lurked in the background, though we did suggest once or twice that maybe she wanted to tone down her approach. While we applauded her fearlessness, we also wanted to make sure she didn't get pepper sprayed. We gently redirected her to a less confrontational script.

"We've got strawberry, blue raspberry, green apple, piña

colada," she'd yell at the top of her lungs. *"Our cotton candy is gluten free, dairy free, soy free, but* not *sugar free!"*

We had more luck when we bought booth space at a local street fair, though the day in question brought soaring temperatures, and we sold more bottled water than cotton candy.

The most profitable venture was when people or organizations would commission the Sugar Sisters for events. We took orders for birthday parties and summer barbecues and even an elementary school dance, which I didn't know was an actual thing. Business was promising, and we eventually upgraded from our small cotton candy machine into a commercial-grade model.

As with the hot chocolate and coffee stand and the lemonade-stand-turned-weird-yard-sale before it, the cotton candy business eventually faded, like spun sugar melting on the tongue. It was equal parts pandemic (birthday parties canceled!) and a venture that had simply run its course. We sold the cotton candy machine, but years later, we're still trying to work our way through that fifty-pound bag of organic sugar.

CHAPTER 9
THUNDA CHICKEN BLONG JESUS CHRIST [36]

"Are you sure this is a road?"

"No," Mike answered, continuing to navigate the decrepit pickup along what might have been a road.

In the periphery of incandescent green, I spied movement, something between a hop and full flight.

"What was that?" I asked.

"I think it was a chicken."

"A wild, jungle chicken?"

"I guess so."

The jungle gave way, and gardens flanked us. We entered a village where children, dogs, chickens, and pigs milled about us as we parked the truck.

"Hello," Mike said to a man who emerged, machete in hand, from one of the dwellings. "Is the chief here?"

With his machete, the man gestured to a makeshift house along a path. We thanked him with excessive smiles. Facing a stranger who wields a two-foot knife compels one to convey good will.

---

[36] *In one of my more interesting jobs, Mike and I worked as behind-the-scenes crewmembers on film and television projects. The following essay centers on a memorable moment during the course of that work and was first published in the Travelers' Tales anthology* Leave the Lipstick, Take the Iguana *(Solas House, 2012).*

Machetes in Vanuatu are like mobile phones in the rest of the world. Everyone has one, kids included. They are for sale in hardware stores, grocery stores, and at gas stations and come in a variety of sizes (My First Machete, His-and-Her Machetes, the Granddaddy of All Machetes, etc.). In a place where the foliage grows supernaturally fast and dense, it's handy to have a large knife with which to hack your way home from the office. We made our way down the path, but the chief emerged from his home before we reached his door, our presence having been heralded by curious children. The chief was a squat man, no more than five feet, with a sizable afro. He wore flip-flops, frayed denim cutoffs, and an unbuttoned shirt with a bright orange floral print, from which his large belly protruded.

"Hello, Mista Mike!" he exclaimed, approaching us rapidly and with open arms.

"Hello, Chief." Mike extended his arm for a handshake, which the chief used to pull him into a bear hug. "This is my wife, Amanda." Mike gasped as the air was pressed from his lungs.

"Hello, Amanda!" As the chief enveloped me, I noticed a tiny green spider crawling in his hair. I debated plucking it out for him or letting him know but decided to let it go. Such creatures were a part of life.

"It is so nice to see you!" the chief exclaimed, then giggled with the bashful *tee-hee* of a little girl.

"I was wondering if we might talk to some of your people about renting their canoes," Mike explained.

"Of course!" cried the chief. "Let us go to the tree!" The chief never spoke without a joyous exclamation point, and he periodically clapped out of sheer delight.

A band of small children joined us and swung from Mike

as if he were a living jungle gym. We made our way to a large metal pipe, about three feet in length and two feet in diameter, resting against the tree. The chief picked up a smaller piece of metal and banged on the pipe, also known as the town bell. While the ni-Van, as the locals are called, emerged and studied us, the tropical heat brought my sweat mustache into full bloom. I dabbed at it self-consciously and began taking pictures of the town's canoes, trees that had been hollowed out enough to float a family from one island to the next.

The predominant language was Bislama, a pidgin with obvious French and English influences. Often decipherable, the chief stepped in to translate when needed. After taking stock of the available watercraft, we left amid a cacophony of "tankyu tu mas," Bislama for "thank you very much." It's hard not to smile when someone hits you with "tankyu tu mas."

"No," I responded emphatically, "tank*yu* tu mas!"

* * *

Film work brought us to this archipelago of live volcanoes in the South Pacific, not far from Fiji. At the airport, my first indication of native life was a group of tambourine-wielding women, clad in dresses of a matching floral print, cheerfully singing their greeting to arriving passengers.

"You don't get a welcome like that every day," I said to Mike.

A shuttle took us to our hotel, where we were again greeted by a chorus, this time a group of tambourine-wielding men, clad in shirts of a matching floral print. This would be our welcome... every day. The man at the reception counter handed us each a cocktail, and Vanuatu secured a special place in my heart.

We spent three months working in various coves on the island of Efate, the one that Cook called Sandwich, scouting for canoes, deckhands, and hardware needed by the film crew. During our stint, the ni-Van trained for an annual relay race circling the island. Half of the competitors I witnessed ran barefoot. Others donned flip-flops, and a select few sported sneakers. The surface underneath them changed from hard-packed dirt to pavement to loose gravel, and the runners, of both sexes and varying ages, never seemed to notice. I can't walk to my mailbox barefoot, let alone run around an island.

While the ni-Van toughened their soles for the relay, Mike's mobility slowed markedly. I thought he was embracing the relaxed pace of island life, but he grew lopsided as days passed.

"Mike, why are you limping?" I asked.

"Oh, I just have a little cut on my foot," he answered.

"Let me see it."

"No."

"Why not?"

"Because I don't want to show you."

"Is it that bad?"

"No."

"Then show me."

"No."

"Stop saying that!" I yelled. "We are married, and you have to show me!"

After two weeks of insisting that marriage vows included a clause of full wound disclosure, he relented. The skin on the pad of his foot and the underside of his toes was simply missing. The raw flesh that remained, along with the fact that he had been walking on it for so long, made me shudder.

"Holy crap, I did not need to see *that*," I said.

"Well, I told you," he said.

The flesh-eating infection detracted somewhat from the island's mystique. Vanuatu flies compounded the problem; they approach cuts and scratches on human flesh with an all-you-can-eat buffet frenzy. Bandages fail to deter them; they swarm over wound coverings and try to crawl underneath. My coworkers were unfazed by this. If *I* glanced down at a bandaged cut on my leg, however, to find a herd of large black flies struggling to burrow their way underneath my Band-Aid and into my flesh, I would frantically swat at them and then wrap my injury in duct tape.

The extent of Mike's injury left him with more than just flies to worry about. Medical staff treated him but warned that if the condition worsened, he would be taken off the job and flown back to the States.

* * *

It was a typically gorgeous afternoon on Efate when I headed toward one of our trailer-turned-offices. Three wooden steps led from the ground to the door. As my right foot came down on the first step, it trembled, and a shudder swept through the entire trailer.

"Crap," I muttered. "I'm getting fat."

The trembling continued and grew, and I knew that, despite whatever weight had recently attached to my buttocks, I did not yet have the power to make the earth shake. I looked around the job site, littered with temporary structures of little foundation. I didn't know what to do. During the six years that Mike and I lived in the San Francisco Bay Area, I had happily managed to sleep through a multitude of earthquakes.

I'd always thought that in such a situation, I'd display clarity of thought and maybe a little bravery. Instead, my mind turned to mush, and my spine followed. *I should be with my husband*, I thought, but then remembered that Mike was indefinitely confined to our hotel room, unable to walk and in hiding from the ravenous black flies.

I looked around for the nearest human. Spotting one of the locals we'd hired, who was moving with what seemed like a destination in mind, I followed him. It turned out he was simply moving instinctively to evade the ground on which he stood, but you can't dodge an earthquake. We looked at each other with wide eyes and fearful grins. I wondered what his name was. If the ground opened up and swallowed the two of us with a belch of finality, I felt I should know the name of my unfortunate companion.

I was too scared for speech, and so was he, until the earthquake ended. As my coworkers emerged to giggle and discuss the excitement of the previous ten seconds, I thanked circumstance that I hadn't been in the port-a-potty at the time, then made my way there to determine how badly I'd wet myself.

A sign on the ladies' room door read: *Toilet blong ol woman.* I peeked over at the men's room: *Toilet blong ol man.* At first, I took *ol* to mean *old*, as if these particular restrooms were reserved for elderly use. I pictured handrails and mechanical toilet seats to lower the user, then catapult them back to standing when finished. And then I wondered where they drew the age line. What constituted *ol*? Was there a particular number of years one had to have lived in order to make use of these facilities, like qualifying for a senior citizen's discount in the States? Of course, *ol* turned out to mean *only*; *Toilet blong ol (wo)man* was Bislama's elaborate distinction of men's and women's restrooms.

I would soon come to recognize *blong* as the most frequently employed word in Bislama. It can translate to *belong* but also any other word signifying possession or a relationship. Instead of saying "John's house," the Bislama speaker would say "house blong John."

* * *

I drove past the Pablik Laebri Blong Port Vila (Port Vila Public Library) and headed for the grocery store Au Bon Marche. On the other side of town was Au Bon Marche Nambatu. Figuring that Nambatu was someone's last name or something significant to Vanuatu culture, I didn't give it much thought. It only took two months of shopping at this store to figure out that Nambatu was, in fact, Number Two.

My mission at Au Bon Marche involved purchasing Tuskers, the national beer (not to be confused with Kenya's beloved Tusker beer). I'd been charged with bringing beer to the crew. We'd reached the close of a long week and received a pass to indulge.

After consuming my share of Tuskers, I crossed the job site and felt the sudden rumble of another earthquake.

"Oh no," I whispered. My thoughts again turned to Mike. He was finally back on his feet, only to be caught in what I suspected was the Mother of All Earthquakes. He stood fifty feet away, chatting and drinking with the rest of the crew. The earthquake hadn't yet registered with them, likely due to beer.

"Earthquake!" I yelled. They looked up, confronting me with calm but confused expressions.

Three ni-Van stood nearby, also unconcerned and drinking. They watched me run one way, then the next, shouting, "It's an earthquake! What do we do?"

"No, Amanda." One of them grabbed me by the arm. "Don't be scared. It's no earthquake." The rumbling continued; I didn't believe him. His companions were laughing at me. I didn't understand.

"It's only thunda chicken blong Jesus Christ," he explained.

I followed his arm up to the piercing blue heavens, where we watched a helicopter fly low over the treetops and out into the sky above the sea.

CHAPTER 10
THE COUCH THAT SWALLOWED ME WHOLE

I know plenty of people who brag about the Bermuda Triangle of missing socks that is their clothes dryer, but they've got nothing on my couch. It's not fancy or expensive. It's not designed to have secret compartments that suck your most precious items into a vortex of fabric and springs. No, it's not designed to do that, but that's what it does.

One Thanksgiving, we lost the remote. It's not as if the remote got stuck between two couch cushions for a few hours and then was retrieved. The remote was gone *for days*. And since the disappearance happened on Thanksgiving day, those days coincided with a four-day weekend with my daughters home from school. It turns out that no one in my household knows how to work the television without the remote, and I found myself unexpectedly longing for the eighties when, yes, you had to *get up* to change the channel, but you could also do so via a large dial, no remote necessary. If my kids were confronted with the television of my youth, I'm pretty sure they wouldn't know how to work it. Whenever they see a pay phone, they point and loudly announce, *"Look! It's from the olden days!"*

In the absence of our remote after Thanksgiving, before we knew to suspect the furniture, we grew suspicious of our guests. Was the gravy really *that* bad? Or had we walked the slippery slope of politics and offended one of our relatives who, in a cheap-Chardonnay-filled rage, took it out on us by stealing our remote? I'm a little uncomfortable writing such words, because now I've given people ideas. What a great way to screw with another person—steal their remote control. You could also hide their phone or car keys, or if you wanted to annoy them but not be quite so disruptive, take the springy tube that holds their roll of toilet paper in place.[37]

In addition to the remote, which we eventually retrieved when we tore the house (and couch) apart—because after a few days, we were really hard up for changing the channel—the couch has swallowed phones, keys, toys, money, hair bands, a variety of writing utensils, books, and enough crumbs that I could probably make a pie out of them.

"But we looked in the couch," Mike said after we located the remote. "How come we didn't find it before?"

"Because it wasn't just *in* the couch," I explained. "It was *deep inside the couch*. There's another world lurking in there. You put your hand down in there and think you've explored all there is to explore in that particular piece of furniture, but no. You have to keep going and pushing through, and there's an entirely different level. It's creepy."

"I still don't get it," he said. "I mean, we already checked

------

37 *I did this once when I was a child. I was visiting my father's home, which was right next to a house in which my stepmother's parents lived. I guess that made them my step-grandparents? In any case, while at their home, I decided I really liked that springy tube. I found it supremely satisfying, so I took it, along with a small apparatus used to roll up a tube of toothpaste, lest any paste go to waste. When I returned home at the end of the weekend, my mom asked me why I had such items in my possession. I told her that my stepmother's parents had given them to me. She did not believe me, but she also didn't turn me in.*

the couch."

I knew then that trying to explain what I'd discovered was futile. Until he'd stuck his own hand in there, and then probed deeper until he was in up to his manly bicep, he wouldn't understand. It's like trying to explain to someone the feeling of relief after filing your taxes or, better yet, why carrot cake is good. You probably won't succeed in convincing them; it's better to trick them into eating it somehow. Then they'll either get it and admit that carrot cake is delicious, or they won't, and you'll forever know that they're one of *those* people, the type who don't grasp the wonders of a good carrot cake. Also, while I hate filing taxes, or more accurately, I hate having to get all of the requested information to my accountant so he can file taxes on my behalf, the feeling of relief when it's finally done makes me want to break out into a succession of Disney songs, starting with "A Whole New World" and followed by "Let It Go."

When I'm home alone, I never sit on the couch. I'll look at the couch and straighten it if it's askew. I'll vacuum the couch, but I will not sit on it. I fully enjoy parking myself within its comforts if I have someone else by my side, someone to grab onto should the couch decide to open its maw and swallow me whole. It could happen.

The couch, in my mind, is in cahoots with articles of clothing that attempt to trap the person wearing them. Anyone who's worn a sports bra likely knows what it feels like to be held captive by this particular item. Dressing rooms should come with panic buttons or pull cords, like they have in the bathrooms at doctors' offices, so that if you find yourself trapped in a shirt or dress or (god forbid) a pair of Spanx, there is a nonjudgmental woman ready to come assist you. Ideally, this savior is also blind so that she can help without seeing the atrocity before her. I can think of at least four friends who have purchased articles of clothing not because they wanted them, but because they ruined them while in the act of *trying* to try them on and decided the best course of action was to pay for the damaged item and leave the store, never to return again.

There are times when I've been trapped in a dress or shirt and taken full responsibility, knowing that it was entirely my fault, because the garment was a size small and I knew, in every pound of flesh on my dimpled body, that I had no business trying on anything in a small other than socks and shoes.

At other times, though, the clothing plays tricks on you. It tries to confuse you as to which opening is an arm hole or neck hole, or it plays really dirty by featuring additional, entirely unnecessary holes, like shoulder holes and cleavage cutouts and missing sections of fabric that should be there to cover your back. Or you get a dress halfway on—meaning you're already trapped in it and trying to figure out the best course of action, be it full steam ahead or absolute retreat— only to discover that there was a hidden zipper you should have unzipped before donning the garment. This is a bit of a tease, because when you're being held hostage by an article of clothing, you know it's all wrong for you and that when you get it off, one way or another, you will never again attempt to put it on. But if there's a hidden zipper, then the seed of doubt is planted. *Well, sure I'm trapped in this dress now,* you think, *but maybe if I'd known there was a zipper and had unzipped said zipper, then it would not only fit but also be transformative. Maybe it would look, on me, like it did on the hanger. Maybe I'd look like that carefree-granola-beach-wavy-model from the* Title 9 *catalogue*. We all know this is not, nor will it ever be, true.

I'm fully aware that being trapped in clothing is real and that the couch swallowing me whole is not real. That doesn't make the latter any less scary. In my mind, the terror and helplessness of being trapped in one's own sports bra is as real as the possibility that the depths of the couch harbor another, equally terrifying dimension. What if a nest of earwigs live in there, but instead of being harmless, these particular earwigs want to burrow into my ears and hatch their babies in my brain? What if every wayward crumb of the last eight years is joining forces with the other wayward crumbs, not so that I can form them into a pie, but so that they can form a dough that will suck me in and hold me there for all eternity? I've seen *Stranger Things*. It could be the upside down in there.

What if the reverse is true? It is, after all, the upside down. What if instead of dark crevices being home to horrors, they hold hidden treasures? Like lost remotes and car keys or a vacuum-sealed, unexpired package of dark chocolate–covered espresso beans? Maybe I'm missing out by not further exploring my fears. Maybe it's like getting out of one's comfort zone and discovering a previously unimaginable level of joy. But probably not.

When my daughters express irrational fears, I think of my fantasies about being swallowed by the couch or how, as a child, I was convinced that robbers lived inside the toilet, and I would never flush, because that would wake them, and then they'd come up through the toilet drain and get me. Because of these and other truths, I never tell my daughters that their fears are irrational. Instead, I offer to go with them when they've left something in the basement after dark and can't bear the thought of going downstairs alone. And when I'm in need of companionship, they sit with me on the couch.

My daughters and I are there for one another. Our relationships are based on honesty and respect. So I was shocked when my eldest daughter recently told me that when she was in the second grade, she decided to run away.

"Why did you want to run away?" I asked.

"Because you told me the weather was going to be nice, and when I got to school and it was time for recess, it was cold outside. All of the other kids had jackets, and when they asked me why I didn't have one, I said that my mom had told me I didn't need one, because the weather was going to be nice that day."

"You were going to run away because I got the weather wrong?" I asked.

"Well, I started thinking that you'd lied to me or done it on purpose. I thought it was clear evidence that you didn't love me, so, yeah, I was planning on running away from home."

"But you didn't," I pointed out.

"No, I got home, and I was really mad, and I asked you why you told me the weather was going to be nice that day. You said that's what the forecast said, but it must have been wrong. So I decided not to run away after all."

Ever since then, I've reflected on how often my kids come home from school and confront me about weather that did not go according to plan. Why does the fault rest with me? What could I possibly have done to give them the impression that I hold sway with Mother Nature? After all, Mother Nature doesn't even like me. On the whole, it seems that my kids trust and place confidence in what I say, so when I get something wrong, it is a contemptible offense like willfully losing the remote or burning a grilled cheese sandwich. I would never purposely mar the wondrous combination of carbohydrates and melted cheese. And if the remote is missing, my money is on (and likely in) the couch.

CHAPTER 11
THE HAIRY SANDWICH INCIDENT

What are our duties as humans? What are the principles that guide us in our interactions with one another? This should be pretty simple. I submit:

- Be kind.
- Help out when you can.
- Do no harm.
- Speak up when necessary.
- Do not leave empty food containers in the fridge, because we all know that's a real dick move.

I like to think that I model basic decency for my children, that I set an example for them to look to and reflect on when they're confronted with their own difficult choices in life. There are times when I feel I've done the right thing, and others when my actions have been woefully inadequate.

Case Study #1: Yelling at Children. I'm not even talking about my own children, but other people's children, children who are strangers to me, and I'm a stranger to them. But really, they have it coming.

There are days when I pick up my daughters from elementary school. This, in itself, is ridiculous. We live four blocks from the elementary school; there is no good reason why I should get in my car and drive those four blocks. Each of my daughters is in possession of two perfectly good legs. Yet I am easily swayed into making the trip. There are trumpets to carry and bulging backpacks to schlep. There are things like heat and rain and snow to contend with. Let's not even get started on kidnappers.

I did a lot of walking as a kid. You'd think that would lead me to toughening my children, but the opposite is true. There's a reason why certain qualities are thought to skip a generation. When I see the pounding rain, I'm transported back to showing up at school with soaked socks and shoes, and the wet cuffs of my jeans chafing my ankles throughout the day. And so, I shelter my kids when they'd be better off hitting the pavement. I give in time and again, and I know it's terrible.

My children are not incapable. Ivy will ride her bike to school without complaint. The handle of her trumpet case barely fits over one of her bike handles, and she rides with the trumpet banging into her leg along the way. She manages the lopsided weight of it with ease, while I would surely topple over to the side.

Emilia, in junior high, leaves before the sun is up to walk in the frigid cold to the bus stop. Of all the horrors of school, the times when I had to walk in the cold and dark to wait at a bus stop with other kids[38] ranks among the worst. Emilia actually chooses this, instead of riding with our neighbor who drives his daughter to the same school every morning. It's sort of like choosing to go to prison when you don't have to.[39]

---

[38] *Classmates whom I was sure wanted to beat me up.*

[39] *Then again, I was always the sort of person who thought prison might not be that bad. You could get a lot of reading done and probably come out with killer arms and abs if you stayed diligent with your push-ups and sit-ups, respectively.*

On days when I find myself parked outside of the elementary school, I am watchful as soon as the bell rings. Children flood from every available exit, and the havoc they'll wreak depends largely on what they've been given for snack that day. I remember eating lunch at school, but that was it. For my daughters' generations, however, school includes breakfast, lunch, and an afternoon snack.

When the snack is an apple, the sixth-grade boys make a show of throwing their apples from a great distance into the dumpster. They don't really care whether or not they make it in. In fact, they celebrate when they miss but the apple collides with the dumpster; the goal seems to be throwing with enough force that the apple breaks apart, creating a firework of fruit. The problem of course is that no one cleans up after themselves. And it is at this point that I emerge from my car and begin singling them out.

"*You!* Yeah, you. I'm talking to you. Pick it up. *Pick it up now!*"

Ivy is no longer mortified when she emerges from the building to find me berating her fellow students. It is expected and accepted behavior.

"Mom, are you yelling at kids again?" she'll ask as she gets in the car.

"Yes," I'll admit. "But I promise they had it coming."

Once, I was sitting in my car watching a girl drink a soda in my rearview mirror. She looked shifty and suspect. I knew, I just *knew*, that as soon as she finished her soda, she was going to drop the can in the bush next to her. Sure enough, that's what she did. I emerged from my car, self-righteous vigilante mother that I am, and marched in her direction. I picked up the can and stood in front of her. "The dumpster is right there. *Right there!* And you're too lazy to throw this away. Have some *respect*. Pathetic!"

The girl said nothing, remained stock still, and looked off in the distance, careful to avoid eye contact. I'm pretty sure that she thought if she remained still enough, she could become invisible. I didn't really fault her for her reaction. It is exactly what I would have done if I'd been in her shoes—frozen, paralyzed, and rightfully afraid of the crazy, chubby, middle-aged woman who was yelling and picking up my trash.

Not everyone thinks it's appropriate to call a ten-year-old girl, especially one you don't know, lazy and pathetic, and I'll concede that I could handle these situations in a somewhat gentler manner. The problem is that I'm not sure that gentler manner exists anywhere inside of me. If it does, I haven't been able to find it yet, at least not when it comes to children throwing their trash on the ground.

I remember clearly the single instance in which I littered during my life. I might have been around nine or ten myself. I was walking through an alleyway after school. A friend was with me. I often walked to the library after school, where I'd spend the next two hours until my mother finished work and came to retrieve me. I held a can of soda in my hand, but I was finished drinking it. What's a girl to do? The idea of littering felt right because it was just so wrong. I hadn't done much that was wrong at that point in my life. I was still a good kid, but part of me wanted to try *not* being a good kid.

"I'm going to litter," I whispered conspiratorially to my companion. "I'm going to do it. I'm going to drop this can." The fact that I whispered and felt the need to talk through my intended transgression is a good indication that I was not yet well versed in the art of breaking the rules.

And I did it. I dropped the can.

At which point a car approached from behind and slowed down to match our gait. The window rolled down, and a woman spoke to me. She stopped the car, and we stopped walking.

"Excuse me," she said. "I think you dropped your can."

"No, it wasn't mine," I said. The one time I'd attempted a life of crime, and immediately I'd been caught.

"Littering is a terrible thing," she said.

"I didn't litter." Denial was clearly the way to go.

"Well, why don't you pick it up and put it here." She held open a small plastic bag. "I always keep a trash bag in my car so that there's no need to litter."

I dutifully retrieved the can and put it in the bag. I was mortified. And I never littered again.

The woman had the gentle manner that I lack. I'm hoping that my bluster and belligerence and, let's be honest, downright insults to the students at my daughter's elementary school don't hinder the lesson. I'm hoping that, like me, having been called out and humiliated will keep them from repeating the action.

But I don't always speak up when I should, which brings us to…

Case Study #2: The Hairy Sandwich Incident. This occurred at a lunch meeting, the particulars of which are unimportant. Suffice it to say that it took place at a restaurant, it was fairly boring, and I don't even recall the names of the other people there. But I remember what one of the men looked like. He was perhaps in his early fifties, slight build and the salt and pepper hair and short beard of an English professor, or a serial killer who's really good at masking their inclinations and blending in with society. We'll call him Dave.

Dave ordered a sandwich. It was a fancy sandwich, as we were at a posh downtown restaurant, at least five of us in attendance. At one point, I glanced over and noted what I thought to be a hair poking out of Dave's fancy sandwich. Would I have said something if I'd known him better? We'd only just been introduced, and I was also very low in rank at this particular meeting. I was there for the free, fancy food, whereas Dave was actually necessary when it came to the boring parts, like knowledge and decisions. For whatever reason, I said nothing. I watched as Dave took another bite of his sandwich. He did so in slow motion. I watched the workings of his jaw and then the slight start as he recognized that something in his mouth was not food. Then the expression change to horror as he realized that it was a hair. He used two fingers to grasp at his tongue.

It took forever.

When he finally had hold of the offense, he pulled, and the horror on his face intensified as he realized the hair was long. It just kept coming. He pulled and pulled, and I could imagine the feeling of that hair with no end being dragged along his tongue. No one spoke of it or acknowledged it. The others kept talking. Dave put his sandwich down. I don't think he picked it up again. It took him a full two minutes and lots of water to erase the revulsion from his face. That sandwich didn't seem so fancy now.

I could have saved Dave from the horror. I could have tactfully pointed it out to him, at which point he could have notified a staff member, who would have immediately removed the plate and returned ten minutes later with a freshly made, replacement sandwich, equally fancy but this time appropriately bald. But I didn't. I simply watched it unfold. I failed to speak up.

I like to think that I'm a decent person. That I do the right thing. But the evidence doesn't always support that. There's a very real possibility that I am a sadist and a horrible human. Why did I not save Dave from the horrors of the hairy sandwich? The only consolation I give myself is that there's a chance Dave actually was a serial killer. Maybe he deserved it.[40]

People can learn. People can change. I might still be a horrible person, I might still yell at children (it's for their own good), but I have never since let someone eat a hair. Never. It's as if it is now against my religion. If you are sitting next to me and I suspect that a hair lurks in your bowl of chili, I will shove you aside and put my entire hand inside that bowl and root around until I either find the hair and remove it, or until I am satisfied that, in fact, there is no hair in your bowl of chili.

You're welcome.

ö Ö ö

---

40 *For criminals guilty of truly heinous crimes, maybe this is something the prison system could adopt. Random hairs in the food, so that no one could ever relax while eating, knowing that a hair of unknown origin might be lurking somewhere in their tuna casserole. Or does that go beyond acceptable punishment and venture into the realm of cruel and unusual?*

CHAPTER 12
HOW TO BE CHUBBY

Note: one need not be chubby to be awkward, which comes in all shapes and sizes. Nor do you need to be awkward to be chubby, as I can think of many chubby people who are graceful and elegant. I happen to be one of those rare unicorns blessed with being both awkward and chubby. I'm special like that.

My weight has fluctuated throughout my life, and honestly, I think that's completely normal. At least it is for me. People who are mystically able to maintain a steady weight throughout their lives might not understand this. (They also might not get what it is to be awkward.) They may make rude comments about your weight gain and/or invasive comments about your weight loss, implying that you are unwell or have likely started a meth habit. When encountering such people, one must give no fucks.

How to Be Chubby: A Field Guide

- **It's helpful to exist during a pandemic.** And you don't have to depend on lack of exercise alone to get chubby. Eating out of boredom and depression will help too.

- **Drink alcohol.** You'll likely do more of this during depressive episodes, pandemics, and election years.

- **Give up alcohol.** To fill the void left by a lack of booze, you'll enter a stage I call Eating All the Things. This will obliterate any hopes of weight loss you might have had your sights on as a benefit of giving up alcohol.

- **Marijuana.** You might think that by switching to Mary Jane to lessen your alcohol consumption, you'll consume fewer calories. This is true only in the short term, because any sort of high will soon be followed by the inevitable munchies. The munchies are real. It's as if suddenly you are compelled to shove All of the Things into your face.

- **Become a human garbage disposal.** I adopted this technique when I became a mother. Out of a misguided frustration with wasted food, I'm capable of consuming all manner of another's leftovers. Half a cheese stick here, a few spoonfuls of macaroni and cheese there, some neglected tater tots, whatever.

- **Get a deceptively flattering mirror.** I have one of these, and it makes me look much trimmer than I am. This provides a lovely shield from reality. My daughter has the opposite, a mirror that looks like something from a carnival funhouse. These should be banned, and I'm embarrassed to admit I have not yet destroyed it.

- **Love thyself.** Be good to your body and foster its health. This should be done with no regard to irrelevant concepts like thin or fat. The end result of this may be a state of chubbiness. It's all good.

- **Own it.** This doesn't mean you have to be funny like the chubby-comedian type. You don't have to be Chris Farley and shake your goods next to Patrick Swayze.[41] You can, however, be confident and sexy and happy while still being chubby. It's so much more fun than sucking it in all the time or hiding behind your hands neatly folded across your belly.

- **Fantasize about activities in which you don't actually engage.** Twice a week, I take my daughters to Taekwondo class, and twice a week I think about enrolling myself in one of the adult classes. Have I done it? No. It could be that I just want a *dobok* of my own. A *dobok* is the uniform of Taekwondo practitioners and consists of white pants with an elastic waist (perfect) and a white, V-necked jacket. Much like scrubs, it's a look that I find universally flattering, and it would be easier for me to enroll in my local adult Taekwondo classes than to suddenly get a job that requires me to wear scrubs. It's possible that neither scenario will ever happen.

- **Find a mate who desires you, regardless of your shape.** Surely, my husband is appreciative when my fluctuating weight fluctuates to more fit and less chubby, but he certainly knows better than to ever give voice to such a thing.

- **Take a belly dancing class.** I enrolled in belly dancing classes at my local fitness studio. My instructor tried

41 *I just realized they're both dead, and now I'm a little sad.*

to teach me what she calls "the truffle shuffle," where you get your belly chub to jiggle in a pleasing manner. I have yet to master this task, but I'm on my way. Belly dancing is a way to celebrate all bodies in their various sizes and shapes.

- **Spend most of every day sitting on your buttocks.** If I was still waiting tables or cleaning houses, I would likely be less chubby than I am at present. This is because the majority of my time is spent writing, which I do while sitting down. I realize that there are things such as stand-up desks, but I feel like when I stand, all my creativity oozes down into my toes, where I can't get to it.

- **Work in your kitchen.** Over the years, I've set up occasional office spaces within my home, but I invariably return to working at the kitchen island. It is simply where I am most comfortable and productive. As a result, when I pause to look up from my computer, I see the fridge, just feet away.

- **Have a sugar-obsessed child.** While one of my daughters loves to express herself through oil paints and digital animation, the other prefers to work in sugar. She is constantly making cookies, cupcakes, cakes, ice cream, and other treats. And she's really good at it. While I try not to eat her creations, I am often forced, kicking and screaming, into the role of taste-tester. It's a tough job, but I always come through for her. When I once attempted to curb her sugar production, she began bargaining: "Okay, fine,

I won't make a lemon meringue pie. Instead I'll make frozen bananas." I agreed to this before realizing that "frozen bananas" means more than a banana placed in the freezer. The banana is first coated with chunky peanut butter and then rolled in chocolate chips. When I learned this, I was both dismayed and overjoyed.

- **Recognize that other people's issues are other people's issues.** If you are healthy, happy, and kind, then the diameter of your thigh or the size of your pants or the jiggliness[42] of your arms does not matter. I know people who default to body size as the primary means of identifying people, even when there are multiple other identifying characteristics, and I find this maddening. Example:

  ○ **Person with Unacknowledged Judging Issues (PUJI):** "That party was fun. Did you meet Theresa? She was the bigger gal." This is accompanied by arms extended to indicate a larger, rounder body than the speaker's.

  ○ **Me:** "Theresa? You mean the one-legged, green-haired ER doctor who performed the Heimlich in the middle of the party to save the life of the kid choking on a cocktail weenie?"

  ○ **PUJI:** "Yeah, she was the bigger gal."

---

[42] *Probably not a word.*

You cannot let PUJI's way of thinking influence you, nor under any circumstances should you ever wonder how PUJI might describe you when you're not around.[43]

ö Ö ö

---

[43] *But if I had to guess… "You know Amanda. She's kind of a bigger gal," with accompanying arm gestures to signify my girth.*

CHAPTER 13
MY RELATIONSHIP WITH DAVID SEDARIS

If you're not familiar with David Sedaris, you should probably set this book aside, or just burn it, and go find something by David Sedaris to read. He's exactly like me, except he's an older, successful gay man, an international literary sensation in the world of humor, whose work is sometimes a commentary on the human condition but always hilarious, sometimes darkly so, and his work has been translated into all the languages. All of them. I don't know how many languages there are, but all of them. He's won all of the awards. Written in all of the genres. Everyone loves him. Everyone. Okay, maybe not everyone, but everyone with whom I can relate. Other than everything about him, he's exactly like me.

I imagine that's how some people feel about certain celebrities. For instance, I don't really know what any of the Kardashians do. Maybe the job of a Kardashian is to be pretty and take pictures of one's butt and share those pictures with the world. I don't actually know. But I know that there are people like that and people who adore those people. They place them on pedestals and have insatiable appetites for more media centered on those people. Okay, I don't feel *exactly* that way about David Sedaris. I like to think that I have some healthy boundaries in place when it comes to my imaginary and one-sided relationships with famous people. For example, I don't need to see a picture of David Sedaris in a thong, showing his ass to the camera while looking playfully over his shoulder. I don't care what he does with his hair or if he perfects a pouty look with his lips. None of that really matters to me, like it seems to matter in other imaginary and one-sided relationships with famous people.

When it comes to my relationship with David Sedaris, well, it's complicated. He doesn't know that, but that's okay. He's super busy being the end-all. Here's us in a nutshell:

1. I stood in line for hours at Hastings, a bookstore that also sells a variety of novelties that are either sexual in nature or could be associated with fart jokes. A literate version of Hot Topic, perhaps. Eventually I reached the front of the line and it was my turn to meet David. I did so. He shook my hand. I wanted to hug him but knew that if I did, I'd probably end up being charged with assault because I wouldn't want to let go.

2. I cleaned houses for a living, and David once cleaned houses for a living. We are both short. I write humor, and he is David Sedaris. Our commonalities are too overwhelming to ignore.

3. My first ever published article came out in *IDAHO* magazine. It's about #1.

4. David came back to town for another reading and book signing. It was Halloween, and I wore devil horns and a black boa. He signed three books for me. One was for my daughter, and in it he wrote, "Your mom looks like the devil." The second was for my

other daughter, and he wrote, "I knew your mom when she was young." The third was for my sister, who lives three thousand miles away. In that copy: "I'm so sorry I missed you." After he signed my books, I gave him a copy of the article I wrote about him in *IDAHO* magazine.

5. A postcard arrived from France. David had gifted me with his handwriting. All the way from France. At this point I knew we had something special.

6. David was in town again. I gave him a copy of an essay I wrote about that time I smoked pot and shat myself at a dinner party.

7. David wrote again. Another postcard from France. He told me he enjoyed my piece because you rarely read about women shitting themselves.

8. I treasured David's postcards. I vowed to keep them safe. I put them somewhere special. So special that I will never see them again.

9. I met someone, and we talked about David. She told me that she once received a postcard from him, "All the way from France." Not a second went by before I informed her that I'd received *two* postcards. Due to the unfortunate events of #8, I was unable to produce proof.

10. I watched David's entire series of lessons on Masterclass.com. I was dismayed when he talked about amateur writers who are always handing him something to read, something that will invariably be

poorly written and self-indulgent.

11. I listened to David's latest book on audio, because his humor is amplified by his delivery. Though we haven't seen each other in years, I feel that the bond between us is still strong. David is unaware of our bond, but I can be aware for the both of us.

CHAPTER 14
THE SHARKS AND THE JETS

Our friends purchased what they call a "baby house" in one of Arizona's many sprawling retirement communities with row after row of baby houses, also known as camper vans, pre-fabs, and mobile homes. The residents of these communities love to decorate their exteriors, maybe because they can only do so much decorating on the inside, so their self-expression is bound to bleed its way to the outside.

There were wind chimes and painted rocks, bouquets of fake flowers and wooden plaques etched with "The Flander Family!" and "Sherry & Ted" and "It's five o'clock somewhere!" People tooled around in golf carts and walked small dogs. I didn't see any medium-sized or large dogs, only small ones. I guess the size of one's pet must be proportionate to the size of one's living quarters.

One resident didn't have a small dog, but he did fashion a cooler onto an electric cart. He sat straddling the cooler as it sped around the complex, and whenever he felt parched, he would stop and stand and retrieve a can of Pabst before taking his seat again and continuing. All of the motorized transportation, be it golf cart or cooler, had little American flags fastened to tiny poles. Some had Canadian flags as well.

The sprawl had five swimming pools and three giant community centers. The spreadsheet detailing the activities one might attend looked like NASA launch plans. It was a complex listing of knitting circles, prayer groups, and mah-jongg meetings. You could attend Spanish conversation hour or participate in shuffleboard tournaments. Scrabble, billiards, needlepoint, yoga, bird-watching, book clubs, and do-it-yourself taxidermy. I might have exaggerated that last one. The clubs in which you are interested say a lot about you as a person, and not always the things you want them to say. For instance, I knew that in such a place, I'd explore the Word Origin Appreciation Society and the Hand Lotion Connoisseurs Club, perhaps even dabble in a group that traded recipes for plant-based home remedies. This is in contrast with the groups I could see Mike gravitating toward: Men's Competitive Pull-ups or Senior Entrepreneurs or the Intermittent Fasting Accountability Partners. Basically, my husband's golden years would be a mix of Richard Branson and Tony Robbins, while I'd resemble Betty White's duller, less attractive sister.[44]

What our friends loved about their community wasn't the schedule for various interest groups but the lineup of live music. They are suckers for a good cover band or, for that matter, even a mediocre cover band. The idea of walking half a block every evening for drinks and dancing had swayed them into purchasing their baby house.

"Your timing is perfect," Rachel said when I told her of our plans to fly in and stay with them for one night before our Spartan race,[45] at which I envisioned myself dropping dead

---

[44] *I have no idea whether or not Betty White had siblings. The sister to which I am referring is entirely hypothetical.*

[45] *See chapter 16: "Spartan Me."*

or at least acquiring a severe disfigurement. "There's a dance that night."

I was confused by the word "dance." Had she said "live music" or "a band we really like," it would have made more sense. But a dance? Would Mike present me with a corsage? Would we get to go to dinner first, like a true homecoming dance or prom? Because that was the real perk of those events, wasn't it? The food?

Or worse, was this a dance-off? Would I be expected to compete in some manner? Everyone who knows me knows that while my husband would be gleeful at the prospect of a dance-off, I would rather cut off my pinkie. I'd even swallow my pinkie after cutting it off. No question about it. While Mike has innate rhythm and an uncanny ability to adapt to nearly any type of music in any situation, I move about the dance floor in awkward, self-conscious jerking that makes me look like I'm in the early stages of seizure. People look at me quizzically, not sure if they should help in some way, maybe put me out of my misery entirely, or if they should nod in rhythm to the music as an acknowledgment and encouragement of the fact that I am, indeed, trying to dance.

"I'll get tickets for you," she said. This added another layer of confusion. A ticketed dance… so, like, a concert? Wouldn't a cover charge make more sense? Maybe they did tickets instead so that if people didn't show because they fell asleep while watching *Jeopardy*, they could still make a buck off of them.

After a short flight from Boise, we arrived at Mark and Rachel's and toured the baby house, which took approximately 1.3 seconds. Though it was small, just enough room for two people who *really* like each other, they also had a finished shed (aka guest room), perfectly suited to house a washer, dryer, air mattress, and nothing more.

Rachel fixed dinner for the four of us, a low-carb meal of lean protein and plants on the side. It's the way in which I truly want to eat and promise myself someday I will eat, just not today. We chatted over a few drinks, though I told Mike that I wasn't planning on drinking at the dance.

"You're not?" he asked.

"I'm just nervous about the race tomorrow," I said. "I feel like I should have a cutoff time—no drinks after a certain time."

Even in my peak condition (which is still moderately out of shape and slightly chubby), I had doubts about my ability to complete the Spartan race. Adding in a hangover was not something I wanted to do.

"Well, let's just see how it goes," Mike said, which I knew meant that he was planning on drinking whatever he damn well pleased. And I knew he'd be able to do just that and then still do that Spartan race as if it was a stroll in the park.

As we walked to the entrance of the dance hall, Rachel said, "We're probably not seated together since I bought the tickets at different times, but we'll figure something out."

"We have assigned seating?" I asked.

"Oh yes," she confirmed. "You'll see."

I wasn't sure how someone could have an assigned seat and dance at the same time, but apparently it was possible. *When you're not dancing, you need to be in your assigned seat. You can't just sit anywhere! You can't approach seating all willy-nilly! There'll be no shenanigans of that sort!*[46]

A suspendered man named Earl took our tickets as we

---

[46] *No one voiced these things, except for an odd, elderly, scolding voice in my head.*

entered what might have been a high school gymnasium. It was Valentine's Day, and papier-mâché red hearts decorated one wall. At the mention of seating, I pictured large, round tables, but the configuration instead had long rows of tables stacked end to end and butting up against the heart wall, so that to get to your seat, you had to sidestep your way down a narrow aisle between two tables. Your partner would have to do the same down the aisle opposite from you if you were seated across from each other, which I guess you could do, and hold hands across the table. There were hazards along these pathways as well, walkers and canes and the ever-present danger of bumping into an old woman's wig and knocking it off her head. I did not want to be that person.

"Don't worry about showing them their seats, Earl," said Rachel. "They'll just come find a spot near us."

"Oh, but their seats are over here," said Earl. "I'll show them."

It was clear that Earl could not abide any deviation from his set task. Take tickets and show people to their seats. He led us down the narrow aisles, and I followed without de-wigging anyone. Our seats were two cramped spaces in a sea of octogenarians whom we didn't know. The Centrum-silver lining was the heart-shaped box of chocolates that clearly came with my seat. It appeared that there was one per couple placed along the table.

After Earl drifted back to his post, Rachel said, "Don't worry about it, guys. Just follow me."

I wanted to grab the box of chocolates. It was my rightful box of chocolates, but I knew Mike would never do such a thing. Neither would Mark and Rachel, who eat fairly clean. The three of them consume egg whites like I consume, well, chocolate. But not only were those my rightful chocolates, I also felt that I deserved them. After all, it was Valentine's Day. My husband hadn't given me flowers or chocolates but instead was making me take part in a race that might actually kill me. I would be the headline: "Boise Mother of Two Keels Over While Trying to Complete a Race She Had No Business Attempting." Or: "Chubby Momma Dies While Trying to Fake Athleticism." My gift to Mike was that I was going along with all of this without too much bitching and whining. You're welcome.

But this was not how Valentine's Day was supposed to be. Attending a truly senior prom and preparing for extreme physical discomfort. I had earned those chocolates. I needed those chocolates.

I reached for them, and a woman seated next to my empty chair shot me a look the equivalent of slapping my hand. As I clearly wasn't intending to sit in the spot, reaching for the chocolates just made me look like I was stealing. I pulled my hand back and smiled weakly.

We followed Rachel and managed to work two extra chairs in at the table where Mark and Rachel had their assigned seats.

For an old person's dance, the music was quite lively. This wasn't a sepia-toned room with couples slowly swaying to Billie Holiday and Glenn Miller[47] arrangements. These people liked to rock. They also liked to stomp. It was quickly apparent that they had their own version of *West Side Story's* Sharks and Jets, but in that banquet room, the turf war existed between the freestyle dancers and the line dancers. The band

---

[47] *I love both Billie Holiday and Glenn Miller.*

was aware of this and played songs that catered to each group in turn. The dance floor would be filled with dancers for a song. The song would end, and the dancers would sit. Then the other half of the attendees, the line dancers, would rise from their chairs and take their places on the floor. It was a very serious affair.

Line dancing, to me, is like saying, "Sure, I'll dance with you, but don't touch me or anticipate any eye contact." When everyone faces the same way at every turn, there isn't too much opportunity to engage with your fellow dancers. As well, most of them stared at their feet the whole time. A few of them had scowls on their faces, leaden expressions that showed concentration to make sure they were getting their steps right.

The free-form dancers and line dancers never came to blows. Not that I wanted anyone to get hurt, but it would have been exciting.

"Do you want something to drink?" Mike asked. "I'm going to the bar."

I'd made it quite clear that I wanted a cutoff point as far as alcohol, but things had changed.

"I definitely need a drink if I'm going to make it through this evening."

I'm not uncomfortable around the AARP crowd. It was more the idea of being at a Valentine's Day dance with heart decorations everywhere and not even getting to keep my box of chocolates. It was the discomfort of having eyes on you because no one else in the room is in their forties. Mark and Rachel had told us ahead of time that at these gatherings, they were always, by far, the youngest ones in the room. They qualified to live in the community, but only just.

We, their slightly younger friends, stood out even more.

The evening ended early. Not because I needed to turn in early to make sure I was ready for the race the next day. Not because anyone in our group got sloshed or danced themselves to exhaustion, but because dances in the retirement community did not go past 10 p.m., lest the non-dancing crowd complain about the noise at a late hour. As well, the band kept their volume muted, because there were strict rules on what the noise levels could be, even before 10 p.m. Upon learning all of this, I realized that while I might view the people in attendance around me as old, this was still the young faction, when placed in terms of the greater population, because there were still many residents sitting in their baby houses, waiting for the dance to be over, bringing an end to what I assumed they considered that doggone racket.

All of this made me question the legitimacy of complaints by old people. When you reach a certain age, do you really just learn how to spin the truth to get what you want? After all, how could a group of people be so hard of hearing, yet be equally annoyed by loud music? Was it selective hearing? If the music had been less Bob Seger and more Perry Como, would the number of complaints have gone down?

I watched the free-form dancers and the line dancers, and thought about those who don't attend the dances at all. I sadly realized that cliques and feuding and various levels of cool do not dissipate with age. With enough bars on property, they probably increase. After all, I've heard that senior living communities are often ravaged by sexually transmitted diseases. When you feel that time is running out and you should therefore do more of what you enjoy, that might occasionally mean doing your neighbor.

I thought of the much more uptight and less alcohol-sodden senior living community in which my grandmother lived on the East Coast. Her days were filled with prayer and bird watching and the songsters group. Were they simply a more pious lot? Or more likely, because I'd only ever been there in the company of my grandmother, who was by all accounts a pious woman, I had only ever been *exposed* to the pious lot—the people who decline the dance invitations and only watch nature shows and devote one entire day of each week to their religion of choice. The drama in her world revolved around food—how the assisted-living wing never received produce as fresh as what was served in the independent-living wing.

In a few decades, where would Mike and I fit into all of this? I knew we wouldn't be buying a baby house, nor would he ever get me to attend dances of the Valentine's variety on the regular. But I also couldn't see us in my grandmother's facility, where you weren't allowed to wear jeans in the dining hall. It seems to me that after a certain age, you should be able to wear whatever the hell you want. And if someone has something negative to say, well, that's when you employ that selective hearing.

As my grandmother neared the end of her life, these questions took up residence in my mother's mind. How would *she* navigate her final years? We offered to build her a baby house of her own in our backyard, but I think the idea of being in such close proximity to relatives terrified her. She's realized that the type of company she most enjoys is of the canine variety. Specifically, she likes small, incontinent, rescue dogs. She's had a series of them. She dotes on them, and their company never results in an unwanted STD.

When I back up a generation from my own and see

myself from my daughters' perspectives, I realize that to them, I am very old. I know nothing of the latest social media apps, and they are constantly having to educate me on the current vernacular. This not only means that new words come into fashion, but also that existing words are outlawed.

"Mom, no one says *suspect*. It's sus."

"But 'suspect' is a word," I protest. "It's a real word. You can't just take it away."

At this point, Ivy rolls her eyes. Emilia looks at her in agreement. "I know," Emilia says. "The feeling is virtual."

"*Mutual!*" I correct. "The feeling is *mutual*."

"Oh, whatever," Emilia says. "You know what I mean."

This is terribly unfair. In the world of teenagers, you are allowed to create new words, chastise your parents for using existing words, and then use other words incorrectly. I like to think that I would never have put my mother through such literal distress, but I distinctly remember rolling my eyes when I was a child and she said something was "awesome."

"Adults don't say *awesome*, Mom. Only kids get to say awesome."

"Excuse me," she said. "But 'awesome' was a word, meaning something that inspires awe, long before your generation made it the new 'cool.'" Though I could tell she believed what she was saying to be true, I held on to my righteous indignation, just as my daughters now hold on to theirs.

However the second half of my life manifests, there is one truth I know for certain—I will never again be shamed out of my rightful chocolates.

ö Ö ö

CHAPTER 15
HOW TO FAIL AT MOVING YOUR BODY

I'm not averse to sports. My childhood and adolescence included a fair amount of athletics, and as an adult, I've engaged in a number of physical pursuits. It's not that I don't try but that I rarely succeed.

There was a brief and ill-fated stint with an adult soccer league. The over-thirty team was full, and I ended up playing with a motley crew of brutally wicked twenty-somethings who routinely picked fights on the field. Those girls were tough. They could have been legendary as a roller derby squad or dropped all pretense of practicing an organized sport and just formed a gang.

I've been through running phases, completing a number of half-marathons, each of which serves as a 13.1-mile reminder that my bladder control is simply not what it once was.

As a Little League parent, I tried to be fairly active and participatory. A coach and fellow parent accidentally[48] hit a line drive at my face during a pregame warm-up. That instance broke my glasses, gave me a black eye that my former soccer teammates would have appreciated, and proved that softballs are not, in fact, soft.

Then there was the time I tried to paddle-board around an island. We were spending a summer in Mike's hometown

---

[48] *So she says.*

of Sitka, Alaska, where we rented a small house on a speck of an island for a month. It was a dated, odd-but-endearing home. On days of good weather, the scene outside our windows was idyllic, even postcard-worthy. On most days, however, it rained for hours on end.

On a day of promising weather, I resolved to take our paddleboard out for the afternoon and get a little exercise. I'd previously paddle-boarded only in our small, protected cove, while Mike had paddled beyond to open water and completely circled the island on more than one occasion.

Mike and I are not a competitive couple. There is no one-upmanship or gloating in our marriage, but we are often inspired by each other. All of which is a tactful way of saying that if he could routinely and *casually* paddle around an entire island, surely I could complete the same journey at least once, damn it.

Today's the day, I thought. *I'm going all the way around.* There was no way to get lost; I'd just hug the shore until I arrived back at my starting point. Most people wouldn't need to voice this strategy to themselves, but I'm notorious for getting lost, and my default direction is whichever way is wrong. I envisioned the headlines:

"Directionally Challenged Woman Lost at Sea"

or

"Idaho Mother of Two Unable to Travel in a Circle."

I left Mike in charge of the girls and took out the paddleboard. Paddling on my knees out of the cove, I reached open water and tentatively stood up. I was *pretty sure* I wouldn't fall off... unless I was thrown off balance by the wake of a passing vessel. Or if a whale decided to breach underneath me; that would be just my luck. Or a sea lion might tip my board just to be an asshole. And if I did fall off, did I know how to get back on? Would hoisting myself back up require upper-body strength, which I did not possess? What if the paddle drifted away? What if the *board* drifted away? I lowered back down to my knees, paddled back to shore, and went inside the house.

"Back so soon?" Mike asked.

"No, I'm going back out. I just want to grab one of the kids' life jackets. I mean, I'm totally fine, but I want to go all the way around the island, and I think I'll feel more confident if I have a life jacket." We had adult life jackets but kept them on the boat at the dock on the other side of the island. It was much easier to grab one of the smaller, child-sized life jackets that were there at the ready.

"Okay," he said. "Good luck."

I set out for another try. With a life jacket, I was sure I'd have the confidence to do it. Chances were that I wouldn't have any interaction with sea life. In all likelihood, the worst that would happen would be that I'd fall off, lose the paddle, kick myself and the board back to shore, and find my way back to the house. Not the end of the world, because in that scenario I wouldn't die.

I put the life jacket on without clipping it. Not out of overconfidence or a blasé attitude toward water safety but because it was a life jacket designed for a seven-year-old girl. There was no possible way I was going to get that sucker closed. In fact, the life jacket was probably good for my posture, as it was so tight on my shoulders that it forced them back, and I couldn't help but think of Chris Farley singing

"Fat Guy in a Little Coat" in *Tommy Boy*. I wondered how long it would take for the strain on circulation in my armpits to cause me to pass out. Or would it just deaden my limbs? Suddenly, the addition of a life jacket didn't mean much in terms of safety.

I paddled on my knees beyond the cove. The water was dark, though occasionally I could make out the tops of giant kelp forests. In places where their leaves reached the surface, I spotted tiny snails[49] clinging to them. What if I got tangled in kelp? Every movie scene of someone being grabbed by the ankle and pulled under or becoming entangled (and drowning as a result) flashed through my mind. I looked back to the island, so tiny when I was confined to it but now like its own country, one that seemed nearly impossible to circumnavigate. I pushed from my mind the fact that my husband routinely did exactly that in about fifteen minutes, start to finish. I looked back to the sea and saw the head of a sea lion poking up about fifty yards away. Something about that sea lion's expression convinced me that it was a complete asshole, as far as sea lions go.

"Well, that was fun," I said aloud to no one, and paddled back to the safety of the protected cove.

"How was it?" Mike asked when I returned.

"Great," I lied.

"Did you make it around the island?"

"Yeah, not so much."

"You look kind of funny," Mike said, referring to the life jacket pinning back my shoulders.

As I struggled to remove it, I looked at my husband and

———

[49] *I wanted to name them.*

said, "If you start singing 'Fat Guy in a Little Coat,' I will physically harm you." He laughed, and I realized he hadn't had that image in his head until I planted it there.

My intention had been to exercise while also reassuring myself that I was still somewhat on par with my husband when it came to physical aptitude and a willingness to test it. Without any sense of competition, of course. But instead, all I'd accomplished was getting my husband to equate me with Chris Farley. I love Chris Farley. But when I think of my husband and the celebrities he most resembles, I come up with Emilio Estevez and Viggo Mortensen. When my husband thinks of my celebrity doppelganger, he's now forever plagued with refrains of "Fat Guy in a Little Coat."

* * *

I have a long and complicated relationship with yoga. I've done a lot of it in the past, and I go back and forth with how much of it I do on a regular basis. Much like how I imagine a lot of people relate to cocaine.

I did yoga for years, then transitioned to hot yoga for years, until getting burned out on it, both literally and figuratively. I was on hiatus from yoga for a while until I took note of a sign near my house for Boise Aerial & Fitness. I had no idea what that meant, but I was intrigued. It made me think that somehow gravity would be employed to improve my physique, and that sounded like a pretty good idea. Ever cowardly, however, I signed up for a private lesson first because I was too much of a pansy to just dive right into a class. I ended up receiving an hour of instruction on aerial yoga, which is basically doing a variety of poses, some of which hearken to yoga, with the assistance of a small hammock positioned fairly low to the ground. The end of every class involved lying completely still in the hammock, a position at which I excelled. I am great at lying down. Resting is my jam.

I generally enjoy the hammock version of yoga, even when I come home after a class to find lines of broken blood vessels where the fabric looped under my arms for certain poses. It's like I was punished with a lashing to the armpits.[50]

Of course, I love the class just as much for the people and their stories. At the end of one class, one of my classmates promised that she'd probably have some juicy stories for us in the near future, as she was about to venture back into the world of online dating. While walking back to our cars that evening, she dropped the bombshell: "I'll have to tell you about that one time I slept with a murderer."

Indeed, I thought.

Sadly, I was soon to go on a trip, and it would be weeks before I'd take a class with her again. When I did, it wasn't until mid-class that I remembered she owed me a good story, and so while standing with one foot in the loop of the hammock and the body in mid-air, trying to perfect an aerial tree pose and attain a state of Zen, whatever that means, I blurted out, "You have to tell me about sleeping with the murderer!"

My outburst was forgiven, and I waited until after cocoon, that final resting pose at which I'm so good, for the

---

[50] *I'm not sure why one would do such a thing, but it seems a viable deterrent, perhaps for children who produce rude noises, like making farting sounds with their armpits.*

rest of the story.

"Yeah, so I slept with a murderer," she said as we put on our shoes, as if that would in any way suffice.

"Was he a murderer when you slept with him or did he later *become* a murderer?" I asked.

"He had already committed the murder when we slept together," she clarified.

"Did you know about it?" asked another attendee, and I was glad I wasn't the only one who was intrigued and needed more details.

"Well, not when I was sleeping with him!" she said. "We hooked up on and off over the course of a few months. I found out later that he and his friends had talked about what it would be like to kill someone. Then they ended up picking up an eighteen-year-old hitchhiker. They took him back to their house, hung out for a bit, and then shot him."

"How did they get caught?" I asked.

"They were bragging about it at a bar," she said.

It occurred to me then that if I spent enough time at bars, chances were good that another patron might eventually brag to me about having committed a murder, as this seems a common method of getting caught. Murderers seem to not yet have clued into this fact.

"The guy I slept with eventually got caught, convicted, and ended up with life in prison," she continued, "because he pulled the trigger. His buddy got twenty-five years, and a girl that was with them got ten years. It was just so sad, all around."

"And pointless," I agreed.

"Wait, I can't believe there was a woman involved in all this!" said the other attendee, who apparently afforded women more credit than I do, or maybe it's just that I have a more extensive knowledge base when it comes to true crime and therefore don't put anything past anyone.

"I have to say," I added, "that I think you really dodged a bullet when it comes to this relationship."

I consider myself a smart person, but it wasn't until writing those words that I saw my unintended and macabre pun.

"Yes," she agreed. "I think you're right."

"Wait," said the other girl, and I was again pleased to learn that her fascination was growing and perhaps even equaling my own. "When you look back, can you see any warning signs that make sense now in hindsight?"

"Yes," she said, though she declined to provide any examples.

Naturally, I felt compelled to give her a suggestion, so I added, "Like, *'Wait, I don't actually like to be choked during sex.'*" The murderer's ex-booty call laughed nervously, which I took to mean I was right on the mark.

The exchange reminded me of another acquaintance who told me about hooking up with a man recently released from prison, and how she'd had to utter those same words: "I don't actually like to be choked during sex." That story had come years prior, so many years that these couldn't have been the same criminal. Both stories made me glad I'm not in the dating pool.

* * *

In addition to aerial yoga, my fitness instructor offers classes like belly dancing and twerkin' hip-hop. Both of these reside firmly outside of my comfort zone, and in a rare instance of bravery on my part, I decided to take them.

Of all the things I'm known for,[51] rhythm is not one of them. But I'm comfortable at my local fitness studio, the aforementioned Boise Aerial & Fitness, don't want to go anywhere else, and am in dire need of more fitness-related activities in my life. Plus, since my studio comes with occasional I-dated-a-murderer stories, it seems like it's meant to be.

Belly dancing celebrates the belly instead of shaming it into submission. It acknowledges that perpetually sucking in the belly is not possible or practical and serves no one. Instead, the belly is accentuated and applauded. This is a great fit, as I happen to have a belly.

At my first class, I was worried that my instructor would perform a belly dance and then command the rest of us to do what she had done. Luckily, this was not the case. She is an excellent instructor because she understands the importance of layering movements, particularly when it comes to the rhythmically challenged, like me. We'd practice moving one isolated part of the body, a hip, a shoulder, the neck, an elbow, before trying to blend more than one movement together.

She employed a similar approach when it came to her twerkin' hip-hop class, though with added twerkin' assistance. She'd show us how to move our parts, but if we couldn't do it, she'd come over and physically jiggle our parts for us, so that we could get the idea of what it was supposed to feel like. After the instructor came behind me and placed her hands on either side of one thigh to jiggle it back and forth, so I'd get the feeling of the movement I was trying to attain, she stood up,

---

[51] *Cleaning skills, language skills, finding items that my family members misplace, active member of the Clean Plate Club.*

lifted her arm, and smelled her own armpit.

"Huh," she said. "I thought I got a whiff of body odor." She walked away without another word, but I knew the truth. I smelled. And not from my armpits. I had body odor from the lower half of my body, and her olfactory glands had unfortunately been in close enough proximity to pick up on it. I wondered if later she clued in to the fact that the smell had obviously come from me. If not, she knows now.

Smelling bad was unavoidable, though, because twerkin' hip-hop took place directly after aerial yoga, and as gentle as that version of yoga was, I still managed to exert myself. It takes very minor levels of exertion for me to begin emitting unsavory odors. I contemplated how to not smell bad during future classes. Should I purchase one of those sprays for people who smell bad and try to spritz the crotch area in between classes? If I double-layered my clothing, would that keep any offensive smells from seeping out or just restrict airflow and thereby further intensify the potency of my odors? I haven't yet settled on a correct course of action.

I was delighted to find that I could mimic all of the instructor's movements when done at the slowest possible pace. It was when she increased her pace and the movement started to resemble actual dancing, or perhaps twerking, that I lost all capability. Nonetheless, I was able to stumble my way through the class and enjoyed it enough that I vowed to return.

Before the next hip-hop class, I put knee pads on my list of things to buy, as we were working on a choreography that included dropping to one's knees. When I mentioned to Mike that I needed to buy knee pads, he suggested I ask Emilia, as we'd purchased knee pads for her the previous year when she played volleyball.

"Here you go," Emilia said when I asked to borrow them. "What do you need knee pads for?"

"Well, I'm taking this twerkin' hip-hop dance class," I explained.

"No, really," she said. "What do you really need them for?"

"I'm serious," I insisted. "I'm learning to twerk, and sometimes we get down on our hands and knees."

"Okay, I actually don't want to know anything more," she said. "And you can go ahead and keep the knee pads. I don't think I want them back."

Apparently, the idea of her mother twerking was a disturbing one.

When the next class was over, the instructor and other attendees began to freestyle dance, just for the fun of it. And that's when I sucked all the air and joy out of the room by standing there, stock still. I made it weird, I made it awkward, and after a few seconds, they stopped dancing. Had I danced with them, it would have been a fun end to the class, but since I wasn't capable of dancing in a studio with other girls to a song I'd normally never listen to, it was like I peed on the moment.

I'd love to say that my excuse is that I'm older than the instructor, and likely decades older than some of the other attendees, but I know that's not a viable out. My seventy-five-year-old mother-in-law teaches Zumba classes. She shakes her booty on the regular and by doing so exists as a constant reminder that I cannot use age as an excuse. If anything, I should be shaking my booty more as I get older. Part of me wants to, and the other part of me wants to continue being the wet blanket that I was born to be.

The aerial fitness studio has become the perfect place for me to move my body, as I've embarrassed myself in many ways. It's as if I've gotten the humiliation out of the way and can now move about freely there. I have no dignity left to lose.

This is never more apparent than during a silks class. Silks are exactly as they sound—long, flowy stretches of fabric that very bendy and strong women and men use to twirl around in, a la Cirque du Soleil. To get airborne and moving on the silks, one must have an incredible amount of upper-body strength. As such, I'm rarely ever able to get airborne or moving. Nonetheless, I show up and try, often spending an entire hour just practicing holding up my own body weight. Watching me in a silks class is as exciting as I imagine working a toll booth to be.

On one occasion, while I did an hour of grunting and hoisting in the corner, an out-of-town visitor stopped by to practice on the studio's two poles. She was a fifteen-year-old pole champion, getting ready to compete at a national tournament. She arrived with an entourage of relatives there to watch, and this young phenom demonstrated that what was once thought of as a stripper's prop has since been elevated to a legitimate sport… for young girls.

I grunted and hoisted and hoisted and grunted while she twirled and inverted and performed many other moves that I'm sure have fancy names. I think that most women in my position that day would have left. We were the only two students in the small studio—me, a grunting, sweating, forty-something blob, next to a lithe teenage beauty. My hips hurt just watching her do the splits while suspended upside down in the air. The fact that she brought an audience in the studio with her intensified my discomfort. But I didn't leave. I stuck it out. Because I may not have flexibility or grace or talent or rhythm or the arm strength to hold my body up for three full seconds, but I do have an amazing lack of shame. And it is truly breathtaking.

CHAPTER 16
SPARTAN ME

"So, I wanted to talk about something…" Mike trailed off. His voice had that kid-gloves quality he uses when he's afraid I might freak out.

"Oh no, what is it? Just tell me," I demanded. I knew he wasn't having an affair, because we spend almost every minute of every day together, so there wasn't time for that.

"Well, there's a series of obstacle course races called the Spartan Trifecta, and I think maybe we should do it."

At least now I had an idea of what we were talking about. A physical challenge. Until he comes out with it, I'm always left wondering what it will be. The possibilities range from "let's try eating nothing but spinach and egg whites for thirty days" to "I think we should start eight new businesses." He's a fairly healthy person, so spinach and egg whites are staples in our home. He's also driven in all areas of life, including business. That's a good thing, but I really think there should be a cap on how many LLCs one can file for.

When it comes to exercise, he's roped me into a number of different routines over the years.[52] In doing so, I've learned that my husband holds his breath when he exercises. We exercise together, so our workouts are accompanied by

---

[52] *Despite the fact that I've literally written the book—or at least a chapter—on how to fail at moving your body. For reference, please see previous chapter, "How to Fail at Moving Your Body."*

my command of "Breathe, Mike," every few seconds. What's remarkable about this habit is that often when he does this, his eyes are wide with panic, as if the realization that he can't breathe is just hitting him.

While I wouldn't say he's obsessed with his physical health—after all, the man loves a cocktail on the deck and sometimes allows himself a bacon cheeseburger—he does pay a lot of attention to his level of fitness. He's an early riser as well, which has forced me to become a morning(ish) person, an identity I begrudgingly adopted. It's not uncommon for Mike to wake before 5 a.m. He'll slip silently out of our bedroom to the back deck and climb into the hot tub before starting his day. Since it's dark at 5 a.m., he usually goes in the nude, no danger of scaring or delighting the neighbors at that time of morning. He used to take a towel and flip-flops, but just like giving up swimming trunks, he's shed these things over time. He walks barefoot and, when he gets out of the hot tub, just drips a path wherever he walks for the next few minutes. I can't understand how he navigates such extreme temperatures—the nipple-hardening cold of the early morning to the simmering heat of water and then back again.

Bolted to the back of our house, next to the hot tub, is a pull-up bar. When Mike says he wants to do something like bolt a pull-up bar to the back of our home, I'm no longer fazed. Because of its location, he decided that when he gets out of the hot tub in the morning, he might as well do a few pull-ups. Should a beam of light from an alien spaceship suddenly illuminate our back deck one early morning, visitors from another planet would likely see my husband, naked and wet, doing pull-ups.

"What we'd do is complete three Spartan races in the

next six months, and that will equal the Spartan Trifecta," he explained.

"So, what are these obstacles like?" Part of me needed to know if it included something terrifying like swinging from jungle vines. The other part of me really wanted to swing from jungle vines.

"I don't think it's anything too tough. There are things like carrying a heavy sandbag and climbing a rope."

"Yeah, I'm pretty sure I can't climb a rope. I haven't climbed a rope since I was forced to do so at camp or in gym class when I was ten." I didn't add that I hadn't been able to do it then either.

"That's okay," he assured me. "You don't have to do them all."

"Oh." I relaxed.

"If you can't complete an obstacle, you just do thirty burpees instead."

"Oh."

I'd already been introduced to the world of burpees, which is synonymous with a world of hurt. If you're not in the know, a burpee is an exercise (as well as a leading seed manufacturer). You start standing upright, then put your hands on the ground and jump your feet back as if you were about to do a push-up. You lower your chest to the ground, then push yourself up, hop your feet up near your hands, then jump up and clap your hands together overhead as if completing a jumping jack.

The beginner version of a burpee is basically this: fall down and attempt to return to standing.

"And how many obstacles are in this race?" I asked.

"About twenty."

"So, you want me to run five miles in a race, and potentially have to do six hundred burpees along the way?" We both knew I was unlikely to survive.

"Most of them you'll be able to do," he said. "And we'll just have fun. It's not like we're trying to beat a specific time or anything like that."

"Will I have to get wet?"

"Probably," he admitted.

I'm not a fan of water, especially cold water and if I have to get it on me. I react much like a cat who finds it suddenly has a wet paw. I hold it away from my body and then shake to get it off me. I wouldn't mind water so much if it wasn't so wet. I feel the same way about sand. If it was just a little less sandy, I might handle it better.

"Is this the same race that your sister does?" I asked.

"Yes, their whole family does it. They love it." Mike's sister is as much into fitness as he is, but she and her husband had also completed the race with their kids. Surely if a family of four could do it, so could I. On the other hand, my nieces were far more fit than I'd ever been.

I relented, because I didn't want to be the lame wife who always said no and was never up to a challenge. I wanted to be the perky optimist who said, "Great! That'll be fun! Let's do it!" Those words never actually came out of my mouth. It was more like, "Fine," uttered with a poorly masked scowl. I don't understand the people who immediately agree to such things, who get excited about them and seek them out. Do they have the same anxieties? Are they just better at masking them? Why do other women look good in tiny exercise shorts and sweat in all the right places? I've worked out alongside women who sweat in neat triangles that appear on the chest and back, while most of my sweat originates on my upper lip (my sweat mustache), from the seam underneath my boobs, and in my crotch.

Despite my attempts to halt time, the morning of the race arrived. "I'm not scared," I said for the dozenth time. This was my mantra. Someone need merely look at me, and I would blurt it at them. *"I'm not scared."*

This was my way of communicating that I was terrified. It's one thing to drop dead from physical exertion in the course of a normal day, but it's another matter entirely to keel over from unnecessary activity that you inexplicably paid money to take part in. What was I doing? Who was I kidding?

Outside the course of a Spartan race, there are volunteers manning stations with replicas of the obstacles. A man with biceps the same circumference as his head will show you the proper technique for flipping a tractor tire. A woman with .000002 percent body fat will demonstrate the hand and foot grips used to climb a rope.

"We have time," said Mike. "Do you want to check out any of these tutorials?"

I didn't, because that seemed like adding on extra work beyond what I'd already agreed to. Plus, at these stations there were people there to watch you and judge you. I guess critique is a better word, but it wasn't something I sought. On the other hand, maybe these people had the secrets to success. Or, if not success, at least avoiding death.

At the rope-climbing station, a man demonstrated how to climb a rope. It was my turn to try so that I could confirm that I could not climb a rope. I'd need a lot more practice than a few minutes just before the race. I also didn't want to destroy my arm muscles before we even started. I gave it a single attempt and shocked no one by… still not being able to climb a rope.

Racers are released onto the course every fifteen minutes.

This staggers the racers so that there's less of a bottleneck. We headed to the starting area, and I was dismayed to see that once an official checked your wristband to make sure you were in the right place at the right time, he said, "Over the wall," and you were to then hoist yourself over a wall. It was high enough off the ground that you couldn't just swing a leg over. You'd have to first place your hands on the top of the wall and then, with the aid of a little jump, press your arms up to straight so that you could swing a leg over. I didn't know if I could do such a thing. Mike had assured me in such instances that he'd be there to help, which was part reassuring and part mortifying. At every stop, would Mike have to push me over an obstacle? Would he push on my ass or roll my lumbering body like you would a giant log? Was that even allowed?

I approached the wall, and Mike was ready with a bent knee that I could use as a step to get up. Stepping on my husband from the start without even trying seemed lame, even for me, so I put my hands on the wall and hoped that when I jumped I wouldn't come crashing right back down. I was delighted to find that I hoisted myself up just fine, but now what? I threw a leg over the wall and expected to come crashing down on the other side. I'd probably break my ankle, too pathetic to even make it into the starting corral. Then again, if I did break my ankle, I wouldn't have to complete the race, so there was a bright side to that possibility. Unfortunately, I didn't break my ankle. I made it over the wall just fine and was therefore obligated to continue.

Once over the wall, we were penned into an area with other racers who had the same start time. I felt a little claustrophobic by all the bodies around me but was pleased that those bodies appeared to come in all ages, shapes, and sizes. It was apparent that Spartan races were not reserved for elite athletes and that I just might be able to complete the race without dying.

Released from our corral, which felt like being sent off to slaughter, we encountered walls to scale and sandbags to carry and buckets of rocks to haul up hills. I was dismayed to realize that I began leaking urine after only a few minutes. I was well aware of the fact that I'd probably wet my pants at some point during the race but didn't think it would happen quite so soon.

At one point, we approached a sprawling mud pit. Runners had to wade through muddy water up to the knees. There was no chance of keeping one's shoes dry. This, too, occurred earlier in the race than I would have liked, and I realized I'd have to complete the rest of the race with mud squishing between my toes.

"Well, at least I didn't have to get my whole body wet," I said after wading through the giant mud puddle. As I have indicated, being wet and cold is the stuff of my nightmares. I'll never be one of those people who jumps into a half-frozen pond in January. Not even for charity. I'd rather donate an internal organ (and thereby lose the weight of said organ) than be cold and wet.

"I don't think that was the full obstacle though," Mike said. We climbed a small hill and saw that we'd simply traversed the Baby Pond. Ahead of us lay the Mother of All Mud Puddles. Not only did the water appear to be waist deep, but a floating barrier spanned the middle of it. Once you reached the barrier, you had to go underwater and under the barrier, thereby submerging yourself entirely. This is usually about the time when I begin to cry. I didn't though, because I noticed a girl who'd made it to the barrier but appeared too scared to go underneath it. She stood shivering and looked at me as I approached, as if to ask if I might put her out of her misery.

"Do you want to do this together?" I offered. "We'll go on three. Ready?"

She smiled but said, "No, I can't do it."

I counted anyway in the hopes that she'd rally. "One, two, *three!*" I plugged my nose and shut my eyes and went under the barrier. I never did see the girl on the other side. It's possible she's still standing there, shivering with her arms folded across her chest.

"Wow, you did great." Mike said this with great shock, wondering who I was, because surely I couldn't be his wife who detested submerging herself in water, especially in dirty water. Not only was it muddy, but hundreds of sweaty bodies had dunked themselves in there. It was a muddy petri dish, home to who knows what sort of bacteria that were likely worming into my brain through my ears.

Monkey bars seem like they're not that big of a deal. Most of us have crossed monkey bars hundreds of times as children, swinging effortlessly from one bar to the next. The first time you cross monkey bars as an adult, it's a rude awakening. Our bodies have grown heavier since childhood, and that wiry strength of youth is gone. The realization of just how badly you can hurt your armpit is startling as your shoulder threatens to come apart from its socket. I learned this not the hard way at the Spartan race, but at the playground when I attempted to play with my kids. I didn't think much of it until I moved from that first bar to the second and realized that I was dislocating my arms from the rest of my body.

At the Spartan race, I knew what I was getting into.

I grabbed the first bar, swung to the second bar, then promptly fell to the ground. The bars were too far apart, and I moved too slowly to make it across. I picked myself up and dragged my dusty self to the side, where all of my fellow racers who also could not cross the monkey bars were trying to complete their penalty burpees. When it came to the rings, I thought it would be much like the monkey bars. I almost didn't even try but saw a girl before me who was crossing them. Shockingly, I made it across the rings and saved myself from another round of penalty burpees.

When we approached the rope climb, I didn't even attempt it. I knew from the demonstration area that I didn't have the ability to climb a rope and get more than a foot off the ground, much less scale one fifteen feet into the air. Mike hadn't mastered the rope-climbing technique, which involved using your feet so that the entire burden of your body didn't rest solely on your arm strength, either. But he's adventurous and loves doing terrible things, so he muscled his way up that rope entirely with his arms, made it back down, and then had to wait for me to finish my burpees.

At the spear throw, you only get one shot. This is to keep people from holding up the race because they'll just want to keep trying. If your spear sticks into the hay bale, you get to move on. If not, you do your thirty penalty burpees. As I approached one of the spear-throwing stations, I watched some of the other racers. Most missed and went to do their burpees. One woman threw her spear, and though it hung limply from the hay bale at an odd angle, it didn't fall. I envied the look of triumph on her face as she fist pumped the air and yelled, "Yes!"

Maybe I'll be able to do that too, I thought. *If she can do it, there's no reason I can't do it. It could happen!* And then I threw my spear, which flip-flopped wildly through the air in the general direction of the target before landing with a thud on the ground off to the side. Mike stepped up to take his turn. I had my eye roll at the ready for when he'd inexplicably nail it, but his spear careened as well (and I felt a secret and shameful moment of glee). We went off to do his-and-her burpees.

I figured that the barbed-wire crawl would be the easiest. After all, I've been crawling since childhood. It requires no incredible reserves of strength. You can't fall down when you're crawling, because you're already down. No balance or grace required. So many other tasks involve holding or pulling yourself up—like vaulting over walls and climbing ropes and hanging from rings without falling to the ground. But crawling *starts* with falling to the ground. It's the one obstacle where you're supposed to give into gravity. In fact, you get to fall down and then stay down. It just takes a little bit of effort to then propel yourself in one direction.

As well, I wasn't intimidated by the inherently hostile nature of the barbed wire under which I had to crawl. It wasn't as if it were electrified or periodically lunged in my direction; it was simply an object suspended above me. *Crawling,* I thought. *I got this!*

We began the barbed wire crawl wet with a recipe of sweat and mud, a perfect canvas for the dust of the hard-packed earth to stick to. This brought to mind an item being battered and fried.

I often think of food when I'm forced into physical exertion:

- If you ever see me running, chances are I'm thinking about hash browns.

- When lifting weights, I crave the homemade baked mac and cheese that I made for my daughter's ninth birthday.[53]
- If I have to do push-ups, I'm likely daydreaming about baklava, cannoli, tiramisu, or bread pudding.[54]

It's as if exercise forces my mind to mentally replenish any calories that I might be eradicating.

As the dirt caked my skin (ooh, cake), I realized that the army crawl we'd practiced in our training exercises was not going to work. Whenever we'd done an army crawl during our workouts, it was on grass. We hadn't anticipated the hard-packed earth dotted with pebbles and rocks.

"This sucks," Mike said. I agreed, then tried to focus on the food trucks that waited at the end of the race.

We looked ahead to see that most of the other participants had abandoned the army crawl technique and were instead stretching their bodies out horizontally, holding their forearms in tight to their chests, and rolling, which of course brought to mind the aforementioned cannoli.

I cannolied my way under the barbed wire, and Mike did the same. It was dizzying, and people had to stop on occasion to get their bearings. It was also difficult for directionally

------

53 *I made this particular dish not because she requested it, but because I secretly wanted to stuff it into my own face. Along with macaroni, the ingredients include heavy cream and $8,000 worth of various cheeses.*

54 *If you're one of those people who doesn't "get" bread pudding, you've not had a proper bread pudding. You were probably forced to sample someone's mushy attempt at bread pudding, which had been further maligned by the addition of raisins.*

challenged people like myself to stay properly lined up, horizontal to the finish line. I'd get skewed and end up moving at an angle, like rolling up a carpet that refuses to stay even at the ends.[55] I'd get off track and then find my head about to collide with someone else's feet. I got so disoriented and off track at one point that I stopped and decided to give the army crawl another go. It was difficult because of the terrain and the fact that the underside of one's forearms is not exactly tough. At least, the underside of *my* forearms isn't. Maybe others have learned to callus that particular area; I can't be sure.

I wondered if I could create a third technique, a new trick to make it more bearable. I tried putting my hands on the ground and pulling the rest of my body forward that way. Not only did it not work well (I might have moved a few inches), but it later proved to be the highlight of the video. Mike, of course, wore a GoPro on his head during the race, because he feels the need to document such undertakings. We had friends who would be doing other Spartan races, and he wanted to be able to show them what our experience had been like. When I saw my attempt at trying to pull my lower half forward by propping up on my hands, it was undeniable that I resembled some sort of large and blubbery marine life attempting forward movement on land. It was then that I knew what my true Spartan identity was. I would not be called The Crusher or Spartan Badass or Destroyer or Girl on Fire. Instead, at that moment, The Mobile Walrus was born.

---

55 *Maybe carpet rolling is easier when you're rolling up a body in the carpet, because whenever someone disposes of a body in the movies by rolling up the deceased in a floor covering, they never seem to have that misalignment problem.*

If you've ever seen a walrus try to move on land, you know exactly the move to which I am referring.

I focused on butter, just to keep moving.

"Holy crap," Mike said when we finally reached the end of the barbed wire crawl. "I thought that would be easier."

"Me too," I said. "It just went on forever."

"And did you see those rocks?"

Later, we'd find all manner of interesting bruises covering our bodies.

I'd anticipated doing six hundred burpees but was pleasantly surprised that I only had to do ninety. Only three obstacles eluded me: the monkey bars, rope climb, and spear throw. It turned out that I was more Spartan than I'd thought, and part walrus, of course. I could flip giant tires and swing from suspended rings and move heavy things. We completed the race in an hour and twenty-seven minutes, and at no point during that time did I drop dead. I finished with an undeniable sense of accomplishment. This was fleeting, quickly replaced by anxiety as I realized that I'd only done the first of three races. I'd done the easiest, shortest one, in ideal weather. The other races would be longer and colder and take place at higher elevations.

Maybe I could join the local Spartan gym, where I'd be able to practice things like monkey bars spaced apart at ridiculous intervals. I'd watch YouTube to learn the rope-climbing techniques and perfect my grip and foot placement. The gym even had spear throwing, and I'd do this in wide-open spaces and with every intention of not impaling a passerby. Maybe I'd train and perfect my skills so that I'd conquer the next race. Maybe I would be amazing!

But wait, who was I kidding? (Myself, obviously.)

My Spartan identity was less Conqueror and more Mobile Walrus. What I really needed was some way of getting out of it altogether.

I needed a catastrophe.

CHAPTER 17
SORRY ABOUT THE PLAGUE

As our second Spartan race approached, my anxiety grew. It would be miles longer than the first and take place in Seattle. We'd also have an early-morning start time. It would be cold. The water would be freezing. And so I wished with all my might for a Bible-worthy disaster, something so awful and far-reaching that it would make it impossible for me to attend the race. I'd employed this tactic on previous occasions, but with no luck:

- I've hoped to be hit by a car to get out of a run, an accident that wouldn't leave permanent damage, but maybe require a day or two in the hospital and a cast placed somewhere on my body.
- I've prayed for tragedy to keep me from having to do a workout.
- I've wished my appendix would burst so that I might not have to compete in a sporting event.

This hoping and praying and wishing never worked. I was starting to lose faith. That is, until the approach of our second Spartan race. This time, I conjured the coronavirus, later known as COVID-19. So, that worldwide pandemic that occurred, it turns out that it was all my fault. Of all the wishing for tragedy to get me out of uncomfortable scenarios

I've done in my life, this was the first time that my wish came true. Now I have to wrestle with the guilt, but at least I didn't have to run that fucking race.

It turns out that I'm well suited to isolation. I thrive in pandemics. This is because I love jigsaw puzzles and plants and avoiding people and organizing my closet, and in isolation I no longer had to come up with excuses for why I'm so lame. The *virus* made me do it.

I'm lucky in that I genuinely like the people with whom I live. There's my husband, who brings me coffee in bed every morning. Not only that, but he returns with the coffeepot after half an hour to give me a refill. My daughter Emilia is endlessly entertaining, like when she asks how long things will be "post-phoned" for and admits that having things canceled does occasionally have its "plus sizes."[56] Her sister, Ivy, is as sweet as the sugar to which she's addicted, and always willing to help out in the kitchen.

We spent a lot of time in the kitchen during isolation. We baked cookies and bread, made butter out of heavy cream,

---

[56] *This comes from Mike's side of the family. They are a tribal lot who often confuse words, sometimes with dire consequences in meaning, at other times merely providing comic relief or minor annoyance. For tummy troubles, they always have Pepto Bismo on hand, no matter how many times I point out the "L" in Pepto BisMOL. Likewise, they're apt to describe a feeling of stiffness as having "rigah" mortis set in. Sometimes they get a word right, but with emphasis on the wrong syllable. My mother-in-law insists that the virus is called co-VID, which is better than a neighbor of mine who, early on in the pandemic, combined coronavirus with COVID. She calls it "The Cova," which is something you can learn more about by looking it up on "The Google." In her spare time, she watches shows on "The Netflick."*

and assembled something called a s'mores dip. The problem with having these things around is that I'm then compelled to put them into my face. I've never been good at moderation.

If you already had a rocky marriage, I imagine being cooped up with your spouse would be hell. All of the little annoyances would be magnified as day after day dragged on. Luckily, in addition to a general fondness within my family, we have a yard and live in a place where you can take walks without being a danger to yourself or others, unlike the densely populated big cities, where people *had* to stay indoors.

COVID-19 turned the grocery store into a place where you could go if you wanted to feel awkward. There are other countries in the world where the wearing of masks has long been a practice, not to keep the mask wearer from *catching* germs, but to keep them from *communicating* their germs to others. A Thai friend of mine explained that this is common when someone has a cold or other illness. It's the courteous way to go about your business in the world.

American culture struggled with this. It simply wasn't something we were used to… being courteous. Since I didn't have a mask when the practice was first suggested, I fashioned a headband as a surrogate. It sort of worked, but it also required constant adjusting and made me realize just how possible it is to sweat directly from one's chin. It seemed that when I had my makeshift mask on, I'd turn down an aisle of the grocery store to find other shoppers all without masks. They looked at me as if I came bearing leprosy. I'd casually move my headband down around my neck, where I told myself it looked bohemian chic. But then I'd round the end cap and in the next aisle find myself face-to-face with a masked senior citizen, who'd look at me with hurt in his eyes, as if I'd come to the store with the specific intent of murdering this sweet old man. I'd scurry to put my headband back over my mouth and nose, eager to demonstrate that I meant no harm. And the cycle would repeat itself, aisle after aisle, past empty shelves where ramen noodles should have been. I was relieved when mask wearing became the standard and we could all just be awkward together.

I did my best during the pandemic not to hoard toilet paper. It's hard to judge how much toilet paper you should keep on hand for a family of four, three of whom are female. I'd never documented our rate of usage before, as I'd never needed to. When running low, it had always been easy to procure. But now I had to walk the fine line between having enough on hand and not being greedy and depriving others. The first time I went to the store when toilet paper was in stock and I didn't buy it, I felt the need to broadcast my inaction for the greater good.

"I'm *not* going to buy toilet paper," I announced to a passing employee, "even though it's there, because I *don't* need it and I'm *not* going to be a hoarder."

I must have startled her with my volume and emphasis, because she stumbled back a bit, then said, "Good for you," acquiescing to my demand for a pat on the back.

The run on toilet paper was unfortunate. Why did no one make a run on other essentials, like toothpaste? Would we all let our teeth rot, so long as we could continue wiping our asses? And who first started the rumor that coronavirus targets the anus?

Months before the pandemic, I'd begun baking bread. When it hit, yeast was suddenly in short supply. On the rare occasion when I bought some, I again felt the need to make a loud announcement to any stranger who happened by.

"Just so you know, I've been baking bread for *months* now."
I wanted everyone to know that I had rights to the jar of yeast
in my hand. It wasn't reactionary buying. I'd been baking
bread before it was cool. Well, maybe not that far back, but at
least for months before the pandemic hit.

As mask wearing became more common, I realized why
being in the store felt so awkward. No one wanted to look
anyone else in the eye, because you could no longer tell if
someone was smiling. If you made eye contact, even if you
were smiling underneath your mask, you couldn't help but
look like a stalker. Instead of making eye contact and smiling,
now you just looked like you were *staring*, and what's ruder
and creepier than that? Still, when I wasn't shouting at
people to justify my purchases, so they'd know that I'm a really
good person, I attempted eye contact and smiling. Maybe, if
I was lucky, I was one of those people whose smile extended
all the way up to the eyes, making them crinkle in a friendly
sort of way at the sides. I don't think I have smiling eyes
though, because anyone who met my gaze widened their
own eyes for a second before quickly turning away and
hightailing it out of frozen foods. It's possible that when I'm
masked and smiling, I just look like a pervert.

During isolation, it seemed that everyone we knew got
a puppy, and not a pound puppy either. No one flocked to
the local Humane Society to see what animals needed
rescuing. Instead, people were buying thousand-dollar dogs
of specific breeds.

Our daughters had long since given up on asking for
a dog. We travel too much for such an animal. I wanted
chickens. Part of it was the inclination everyone felt to

suddenly become a homesteader. I had plants sprouted from seeds that I doted on, trying to keep them alive long enough so that they could be transplanted to the garden, where they'd hopefully yield a bounty of vegetables, but would more likely wither and die, because I have wonderful intentions but too often cut corners.

If we added chickens to our yard, we could have fresh eggs and cross one more item off of the grocery list. I'd already researched how to care for chickens and knew of three people in our neighborhood who'd be willing to care for them when we're out of town. The problem was convincing my husband of this. On the one hand, eggs rank as one of his favorite foods. On the other hand, they come from chickens. He's put off by—and maybe even scared of—chickens. It's the awkward, darting movements, or maybe the fact that the animal is soft and feathered but capped at one end by a sharp beak and at the other with gangly, prehistoric feet. He is not a fan.

Not only did I want chickens for the eggs and to take a minuscule step in being more self-sufficient, but I figured they would also suffice as pets for our children, who continued to lament how cruel we were for denying them a dog.

My attempts to talk Mike into getting chickens included a clever list of names, like Eggsmerelda and Benedict and Mikey Jr. I showed him chicken coops online that we could purchase and have delivered, quaint little structures that weren't eyesores and would produce his favorite food daily.

In my mind, not only would the chickens produce eggs and make delicate little clucking noises, chirps and coos that would bubble up from the coop, but they would also love me. I imagined that there would be one in particular that would be *my* chicken. It would get excited when it would see me coming and waddle happily to the door of the coop. I'd pick it up, and it would settle contentedly in my arms, as if it spent all its time pining for when we might again be reunited. This chicken and I would have a special bond. Mike and the girls would be jealous, wondering why they couldn't Snow White the animals quite like I could.

While chickens do have personalities, part of me understood that this scenario was unlikely. I wouldn't end up in a viral video, like those I've seen of the woman who made friends with a bee or the diver who cuddles with an eel. More likely, I'd end up being scared of the chickens and scatter their feed at them from afar. I'd have ornery birds that would peck at my shins and try to make a break for a neighbor's yard, even a neighbor with dogs, because my chickens would be desperate to get away from me.

I guessed that I'd never know for sure, because you can't realize the scenario if you never put yourself in that position. You'll never cuddle with an eel if you don't first put on your dive gear.

My mother is far more Snow White than I am. It's not that birds and squirrels are drawn to her delicate, genteel nature. It's that she feeds them. So much and with such patience that she has squirrels eating from her hand.

In times of uncertainty, people often look for ways to care for other living things. I think that's why so many people got puppies. They were cute, fluffy, distractions. You could love them, and they might love you back.

Since we'd ruled out dogs and Mike was still apprehensive about chickens, I turned to plants. Sure, you can't really cuddle with them, but sometimes they do produce food, and they still count as living things. Also, they don't require you to pick up their poo, they don't eat your shoes, and they are never the cause of finding fur in your food.

I sprouted seeds for tomatoes and squash, hot peppers and eggplant, and pumpkins and watermelon. I saved apple seeds from lunch and sprouted them in the fridge to grow tiny apple trees. I tested every avocado pit until I found ones that took root. I put sprigs of basil and rosemary and thyme in glass jars of water on the windowsill until tiny roots began emerging from their stalks.

The inclination to grow and cultivate is what happens when all my plans are canceled. I clutter the house with all manner of roots and leaves in an effort to breathe more life into the space around me. Of course, about half of everything I grow dies in short order. Orchid leaves turn yellow and limp. Avocado pits end up decaying more than they sprout. And seedlings that I intend for the garden begin to falter after showing a promising start. *What did I do wrong?* I ask them. *Did I not love you enough?* Instead of answering me, they just die. Assholes.

Maybe the inclination to care for other life, which I believe is a basic foundation of being human, unless you're a serial killer, is amplified when the news becomes extra depressing. It's a means of fighting back against endless reports of mounting death tolls and the spread of a virus that we don't know how to stop. Maybe, in my case, I wanted to bring some life into the world because I knew, deep down, that the plague was all my fault.

CHAPTER 18
CHICKEN FEET ARE HOT

A situation is never as certain as we imagine it to be. The pandemic wore on, and not only did we add an enormous greenhouse to our backyard, the assembly of which was like a two-week-long IKEA-born test of our marriage, but we also added a chicken coop.[57] The greenhouse afforded me even more space in which to kill plants. And the coop gave me space in which to (hopefully) not kill chickens.

There are two truths when it comes to chicken-obsessed women. The first is that they love their chickens fiercely.

The second is that they will do anything to convince themselves that their chickens love them back. Don't get me wrong. There are plenty of amazing human-chicken bonds. You can watch endless videos of chickens cuddling with their keepers, riding around happily on shoulders. But when this isn't naturally the case, chicken women will tell fantastic lies to themselves to make it seem so.

Lie #1: when I hold my chicken like a baby, she falls asleep in my arms. Now, it's true that if you flip a chicken onto its back and hold it in your arms as you would a baby, eventually its eyes will close. However, this is not due to the

---

[57] *I'm still not sure what caused Mike to acquiesce; whatever it was, I'm thankful for it.*

hen drifting contentedly off to sleep but because the bird is being deprived of oxygen and passing out. Chickens are not meant to be on their backs. Have you ever seen a chicken flop over on its back and take a little nap? No. If you think you saw such a thing, the more likely scenario is that the bird keeled over and died. But so strong is the desire of the hen keeper to believe that her chicken wants nothing more than to fall asleep in her arms, that she'll routinely flip birds over so that they pass out and she can continue with her delusion.

Lie #2: my chickens squat for me so that I can pick them up. When you approach a chicken and it realizes it won't be able to run away, it may slightly spread its wings and hunker down close to the ground. If you look closely, you'll notice this is accompanied by a look of panic. It's true, chickens are very capable of displaying emotion. You wouldn't think so, until you see a chicken with an expression of true fear. And this is the expression chickens have when they squat low to the ground. They're not trying to make it easier for someone to pick them up. They are either squatting as a sign of submission, assuming the mating position because they think you might be a rooster, or squatting to obtain a defensive position from a predator attack. These are the only reasons chickens squat. They're not hoping you'll pick them up.

Like any living creature, chickens come with a host of possible maladies of which you are completely unaware until you become a chicken owner. Chicks, for instance, can get pasty butts, and you need to identify said pasty butts and clean them or de-paste them. Hens can become egg bound, among other things. This is basically the equivalent of getting an egg stuck in the chute. Apparently, an Epsom salt bath can help. To date in my chicken ownership, I have not had to draw a bath for any of my chickens, but I certainly will if the need arises. When chickens are hot, they pant just like dogs do, but with their beaks open because that's what the little dinosaurs have.

When I say that chicken feet are hot, I'm not referring to some sort of spicy Asian delicacy. What I mean is that when you hold a chicken or have a chicken sitting on your lap (because that's what happens when you become a crazy chicken lady), the amount of heat radiating from the chicken's feet is startling. Maybe that's common to birds in general, but in any case, they're quite warm.

Perhaps the most surprising thing about chickens, which I didn't fully grasp until I saw it in action, is what assholes they can be. I now fully understand the term *pecking order*. Chickens are more cliquish than seventh-grade girls. I won't say meaner, though, because seventh-grade girls can be pretty mean. Chickens form gangs, and there might be a hen who is in with a crowd one day but then finds herself ostracized the next. Who knows what she might have done to cross the other hens? Did she hog the most desirable nesting box? Did she shit on the feeder? Or eat a bug that another chicken was saving for dessert? Whatever the case, chickens will bully the outcasts, peck their feathers out, and probably say some truly awful things, only I can't be sure because I don't speak chicken.

Despite all of this, I love my chickens. Maybe I love them a little bit less in the summertime because I'm not willing to withstand the hundred-degree heat to spend time with them. That's not true. I still love them, just from the comfort of my air-conditioned home. Maybe they can still feel my love, radiating along with the triple digits all the way to their coop.

When it came time to source chickens, as with many of our undertakings, we did so at the wrong time of year. Both our chicken coop and our greenhouse were ready for chickens and plants, respectively, in late summer. This is not when chickens and plants are readily available or most suited to planting. But I lucked out when I stumbled across an ad for chickens for sale in a neighboring town. The chickens had a lot of words used to describe them, some of which I still don't understand, but that included "bantam" and "pullet." Bantam hens are more petite than your standard-sized chicken and produce slightly smaller eggs. I saw Mike's mouth turn down at the corners when I told him of this, and I could see his thought process. *I finally agreed to chickens, and I've put all of this time and money into this goddamned chicken coop, and we're going to get puny eggs?*

Pullets refers to the age of the chickens. They're like teenagers, past the chick stage, so less likely to die or need you to clean off their pasty butts, but not yet grown and to the point of laying their first eggs. Pullets sounded great to me. Also, they were the only chickens I could find.

I responded to the ad and set up a time to go see the chickens. I took Emilia and Ivy with me, and we drove to Nampa, Idaho. When we neared the address of the home, I knew we were close because I could hear a rooster. We parked and walked to the front door, and I realized I was standing on the threshold of a hoarder's home. The tiny front patio of the duplex was crammed with broken playpens, flat bicycle tires, shards of what used to be a terra cotta plant pot and headless baby dolls. With both fear and intrigue, I waited for the door to open. What must the *inside* of this home look like?

Sadly, thankfully, a woman emerged from around the side of the house and said hello. This was the crazy chicken hoarder lady, and she beckoned us to follow her around the outside of the house to the fence line of her yard. There would be no entering of the home where I'd try to take snapshots with my mind to study and analyze later. But as we peered over the fence into her tiny backyard, I found it as visually stimulating as anything I might have imagined. It was a typical pit of detritus: broken toys and lawn mowers, an old fridge, the skeleton of what once served as bunkbeds. But the entire scene was decorated with chickens. A rooster perched here, a pair of hens snuggled together in the dirt there. And the chickens, of course, had zero complaints about their surroundings, like the presence of a standing fan that might have functioned three decades ago or a stack of old tires. For the chickens, these were all useful and interesting surfaces on which to perch, preen, and shit.

Fascinated by the yard, in the middle of which stood a girl of about six, holding and petting a hen, I struggled to focus on the words of the crazy chicken lady, who was telling me about the birds I'd come there to possibly purchase. I was drawn by her appearance. Facial sores, missing teeth. But she spoke passionately about her chickens and used words of praise and kindness when addressing her daughters, of which I now saw there were two. In five minutes' time, it became clear that my new friend's life was dominated by three main influences: drugs, her daughters, and her chickens. Despite the state of her property and her own appearance, which I could delicately describe as "rough around the edges," both her daughters and chickens appeared extremely well cared for.

With urging from Emilia and Ivy, who largely hung back

and just observed the train wreck of a situation, I agreed to buy the chickens, offering to pay more if she could hold them a little longer for me until our chicken coop was finished. She agreed, and over the next six weeks, she sent me reassuring updates about how the chickens were doing, with the occasional concerning text: *If you can't pick them up when you said you would, I'll refund half your money and I'll have to list them for sale again, because I need to make room for my flock.* This was unnecessary, because I'd never deviated from our agreed-upon plan, and I assured her I'd retrieve them just as promised and as soon as possible.

One of her texts announced that one of the chickens had laid her first egg and that it was a beautiful light green color. I was excited and shared this news with Mike, who once again took on an expression of dismay. *Great, all this work for puny green eggs.* He stewed on this for a minute before I could tell that it had become so bothersome that he needed to say something about it.

"Green eggs? The eggs are green? I don't think I want to eat green eggs."

I imagined him picturing Dr. Seuss's green eggs illustrations.

"The inside of the egg is just like any other egg," I assured him. "It's not going to taste any different. It's just that the outside shell is going to have a little bit of a green tint to it."

I could tell he wasn't convinced and wouldn't be until I served him up a plate of delicious, fresh, organic eggs that came from our backyard chickens, at which point he'd be hooked for life.[58]

-----

[58] *This happened exactly as predicted.*

When we went to get the chickens, I had two large cardboard boxes in which to transport them back to our home. The chicken lady's daughters handed me the birds one by one over the fence, all eight of them I'd agreed to purchase, because city regulations limited me to six, so eight seemed like a good number. It was an odd sensation, being handed a bird when you have no prior chicken experience, but I did my best to place them into the cardboard box, one at a time, four in each box. Until I lost my grip on a feisty one and it escaped, which paved the way for the others to escape, and before I knew it, there were chickens in flight all around me. I figured that was the end of it, that the chickens had won their freedom and would now become wild chickens roaming in packs around the subdivision, but it turns out chickens are homebodies. Most of the time, they have zero inclination to run away. Instead of trying to escape, the chickens simply hovered near the fence, because they wanted to be back in the familiarity of their yard. Crazy chicken lady and her daughters helped me retrieve them all.

Emilia and Ivy did their best to speak soothing words to the chickens in the cardboard boxes on the way back to our home, but those words offered little consolation, because they were spoken to chickens. As such, the birds made the journey in a state of distress, but none of them died of a heart attack, so I took that as a win. We got home and opened the cardboard boxes so they could explore their new coop and chicken run. It took a while for them to relax and start checking things out, but eventually they did so. I was happy to see them happy, and only slightly dismayed to see that none of them made use of the chicken toys I had ready for them, including a chicken swing and a chicken xylophone. This is the same as a regular xylophone but hung against the wall of a chicken run. The idea is that they happily and curiously peck at the keys of the xylophone, but we're a solid two years in at this point, and I'm still waiting for that to happen.

We marveled in those early days at how quiet the chickens were. They waddled around making delicate little cooing sounds, but that was about it. *What good fortune*, I thought, *that we have such lovely, quiet little hens*. When they eventually began laying eggs on a regular basis, which took another four months, leading me to believe that the green egg the crazy chicken lady had found had been mistakenly attributed to one of my birds and had in fact come from one of her other hens, everything changed. My chickens now wail with abandon. They squawk and cackle and belt out ungodly sounds. For hours on end. Personally, I find it amusing. Mike feels a little more self-conscious about the noises that now emanate from our yard. He goes through phases of worrying about the neighbors. I remind him that we've been surrounded by barking dogs for the last fifteen years (I have zero guilt about the noises coming from my admittedly loud birds).

We started with eight chickens, including two Frizzles. Crazy chicken people know what Frizzles are, but if you don't, let me enlighten you. A Frizzle is a chicken with a genetic defect that causes its feathers to grow pointing out the wrong way. Sort of like hair that grows in a different pattern because of a cowlick. Only it occurs all over their little chicken bodies. The result is endearing, as they look like extra fluffy chickens.[59]

---

59 *This doesn't harm the chicken in any way, though I've heard you never want to mate two Frizzles, because the result will be a Frazzle, which is a chicken with no feathers at all.*

Of our two Frizzles, one was named Miss Frizzle, after the character voiced by Lily Tomlin from *The Magic School Bus*. And the other Frizzle we named Curry, both an homage to curried foods, including chicken curry, and also as a tribute to Tim Curry, whom I adore. Much like my relationship with David Sedaris, Tim is unaware of our connection.

Unfortunately, one day Curry flew up to the fence and, while perched there, peered down into the neighbor's yard and found it worthy of exploration. This is why chickens should always trust their instincts to stay close to home. Only a second after landing in the neighbor's yard, Curry was seized and dispatched by the neighbor's dog. I like to believe it was a quick death. I was working in the yard at the time and, upon hearing a loud squawk, peered through the fence to see Curry firmly in the mouth of our neighbor's dog, who trotted happily away with his find. Though it was the end for Curry, that dog looked like it was living its best life.

After that, I learned how to clip my chickens' wings. This doesn't hurt them at all and is akin to trimming one's nails. It does, however, keep them from being able to fly, to places like the high fence separating my chickens from certain death.

"So, you're keeping them from getting to the fence so they can't go over to the neighbor's yard," Mike said, "but you're also taking away their ability to fly, or their ability to escape from a predator if they need to."

"You're not helping," I pointed out.

More so than the neighbor's dog, I worried about raccoons and possums and other creatures I'd been delighted to see before becoming a chicken owner. I think raccoons, for all the trouble they cause, are strikingly pretty animals. Trash pandas, sure, but also beautiful. It doesn't matter how ugly or destructive the animal, if it isn't something I get to see on a daily basis, I'm ecstatic to encounter it, like most people would feel when winning the lottery. We once had a young owl perched on the light outside on our deck, and for months after, I would show acquaintances and strangers alike the picture on my phone of the owl who had paid us a visit. I wanted to name it, make friends with it, have it visit me regularly and perch on my shoulder. It never came back.

That's a good thing though, because now if an owl visits my backyard, it is likely because it has its large, wise eyes on my chickens. I once ran leaping into my yard, screaming *"NO!"* and flailing my arms when a hawk did a low swoop in the hopes of snagging Miss Frizzle for a midday meal.

In addition to Miss Frizzle and Curry (rest her soul), we had a list of names ready to assign the other chickens. Possibilities included, as previously mentioned, Benedict and Eggsmerelda and Mikey Jr., but also Florentine and Renaldo and Pot Pie. The problem is that, aside from the Frizzles, the chickens bear a striking resemblance to one another. The inability to tell them apart is a hindrance when it comes to assigning them names. Any good chicken mama would correctly assume that I'd be able to tell them apart if only I spent more time with them. Of course, those same people might insist that, as evidenced by their helpless birds passing out in their arms because of oxygen deprivation, their chickens love them dearly. That same chicken, could it speak, might beg to differ.

CHAPTER 19
ONLY GOD CAN FUDGE ME

*D*oes *her tattoo have the word* fudge *in it?*
I inched closer.

Fudge me.

It said something about…

…fudge me.

That can't be right.

Can it?

We stood in a foot of water at the edge of a lake. This was my first group-camping trip. Friends had invited us. Those friends had invited other friends as well. But those other friends also invited other friends, who invited other friends and relatives. The result was a colony of adults and kids camping along a reservoir. The *fudge me* lady represented the greatest degree of separation between me and any other member of this group. I wasn't even sure of her name.

But gosh, I thought, *if she has a tattoo with the word* fudge *in it, she must have a great sense of humor.* The top of her swimsuit obscured my full view of the words along her upper back. I decided I had to ask.

"Excuse me, I'm trying to see your tattoo. What does it say? Something about fudge?" I smiled as disarmingly as possible.

"Oh, no," she said. "The artist just kind of made it look wrong. It says judge, not fudge." She held her swimsuit straps aside so I could see the full tattoo, which read *Only God*

Can Fudge Me. I mean, *Only God Can Judge Me.*

The lettering of the tattoo wasn't poorly executed, but the selection of a flowery script combined with an unfortunately located freckle spelled disaster. Or, in this case, fudge.

"Oh, yes. I see it now," I said.

"Yeah," she said, "so, you know, fuck off."

She smiled and laughed.

Wow, I thought. *This chick is impressive.* I'd never been told to fuck off in quite such a masterful manner. She had a way of laughing and smiling as she said the words. She even nudged me like we were old friends sharing a joke. But the meaning was clear.

A little while later, I found myself floating on a raft, which was tied to three other rafts. All the moms of the camping group piled in to float lazily and without children, while the dads took over the parental duties on shore.

Everyone had a beer in hand, and half of the moms also had their vape in the other. If you haven't seen a vape up close, the contraption looks like a little designer crack pipe. Or perhaps a stylish plastic tampon. Though it's harder to reconcile the image of someone sucking on a plastic tampon than a crack pipe.

In any case, about half of the women had them. I wasn't really bothered by this. It doesn't emit the same odor that cigarettes do, and if my kids asked about it, I'd just tell them that some of the women took comfort in sucking on stylish plastic tampons.

At some point, my new BFF, the one who has an exclusive arrangement with God when it comes to fudging, took over the conversation. She became very emotional while discussing her relationship with her fiancé. One of the difficulties of the relationship was that the lucky man was behind bars. She'd met him while visiting her brother while *he* was behind bars. Which isn't that atypical, if you think about it. Because basically that's just like dating your brother's roommate.

"But it's not his fault," she explained. "He stabbed some drug dealer in the throat, but he didn't even know the guy. He wasn't involved."

She paused to cry and vape and drink.

This made me question how I define the word "involved." I think when you stab someone in the throat, you are automatically involved, whether you want to be or not. And if they had no prior involvement, why the stabbing? Is this how people with no connection between them greet each other these days? Or did this man have a problem of stabbing random strangers in the throat, and this particular stranger turned out to be a drug dealer?

So many questions.

"And I know he's a violent man. And I worry how my choices will affect my children." She had a preteen and a four-year-old, who were thankfully back on shore and out of earshot. The fact that she felt some concern for how this would affect her children seemed a good sign. But of course, she ruined it by continuing to speak.

"But even though he's a violent man, he's never been violent to women."

I wanted to interject, "Well, he's never been *convicted* of being violent toward women," but thought better of it. She might try to stab me in the throat with her vape.

"We've been together for six years, and we have two more to go before he gets out. And the only reason this relationship has worked is because I'm so loyal."

"So, you two just get to see each other on conjugal visits?" asked my friend, the one who had invited us on the camping trip and was increasingly feeling embarrassed that she had done so.

My BFF stopped crying and laughed, the same way she laughed when telling me to fuck off earlier in the day. "Oh, we don't get conjugal visits."

"Then how did you get your four-year-old?" my friend asked.

"I cheated on him." She was serious and somber again. I, too, strove for serious and somber, struggling not to remind her that she'd attributed their relationship "success" to her loyalty, not twenty seconds prior.

Eventually, we made our way back to shore, the sane ones among us waiting for Ashton Kutcher to pop out from behind a camper and let us know that we'd been Punk'd.

When we reached the shore, we were invited to try the Shaken Baby. This is a drink, not an abused child, but I feel the same way about the term "Shaken Baby" for a drink as I do about "wife beater" for an article of clothing. Is it funny? I mean, I'm okay with things that are wrong, even multidimensionally wrong, but they have to be funny too. When it comes to shaking babies or beating wives, I don't know, I just need an additional play on words or something. I guess I'm hard to please that way.

I'm equally unimpressed with names of drinks like Sex on the Beach or Pink Panties. I get that they're sexual; it's not really… subtle.

In any case, the drink in question is in a gallon-sized glass jar that is shaken and passed around the group and shaken some more. You don't need to shake it violently, and the shaker more resembles a concerned parent than a child abuser when in charge of the jar, but I guess the name Soothed Baby wouldn't be as seductive for the general public, which is apparently really hot for child abuse.

My BFF approached the shore but was still in a foot of water when a guy from the group approached her and held up the jar for her to take a sip. I shuddered with the realization that the jar would be passed around for everyone to drink from. I'm pretentious and hygienic that way.

Given my BFF's emotional state a few minutes before, I couldn't help but view giving her tequila a lot like pouring lighter fluid on a fire. The guy holding the jar realized she was going to need to hold the jar herself. Her preteen stood off to the side. Her dilemma, one we've all faced of course, was that she wanted to get a drink from the jar, but she held her beer in one hand and her vape in the other. And she was standing in water, so she couldn't set them down. At that moment, she needed a third hand. Then she looked at her preteen and realized that this is precisely why we have children. But the preteen didn't jump to attention quickly enough, so my BFF barked at her. "Hold my *fucking* beer!" When addressing her child, she didn't have much of the finesse she'd had when telling me to fuck off, but really, the kid deserved it. I mean, shouldn't she have immediately known to hold her mother's vape or shitty American beer so that mommy dearest could drink sugary booze from a large vat? Duh.

The twelve-year-old calmly took her mother's beer, set it on the bank, said, "There's your beer," and walked away. Her reaction was practiced; I sensed she'd perfected the art of extracting herself from such confrontations to avoid a slap across the face.

But here's the silver lining, because I know that you need it right now: that child looked at her mother with disdain. And there's a chance she was weighing her options, realizing that she had a choice to make of who she wanted to be.

I spent the rest of the trip considering the falsehood of my BFF's tattoo. Not just the *fudge me* part but how she intended it to read. Because in addition to the possibility of being judged by God, if that's your belief, you can also be judged by friends, neighbors, strangers, the justice system, and your own children. Her tattoo was nothing more than a fuck you to the world, indiscreetly couched in religious pretense.

It's not fashionable for moms to judge other moms for how we feed, school, and scold our kids. I think that's a good thing, because parenting is hard, it's a different experience for everyone, and we do the best we can. But when you snap at your kid to hold your fucking beer, I'm sorry, judgment is creeping in. Followed closely by pity for all involved. I am certain that this wasn't the first time the twelve-year-old had been screamed at to hold mommy's fucking beer. I'm certain she's endured much worse. I'm certain the same is true, and will continue to be true, for her younger sister.

Am I unfairly judging someone with a difficult lot in life? Maybe. But if you tell me to fuck off and then hand me a platter overflowing with material I could never dream up on my own, chances are I'll write about it. It's possible this will come back to haunt me. But life is short regardless, so in the meantime, pass the fudge.

ö Ö ö

CHAPTER 20
OVERSERVED

"Well, look who's a member of the Clean Plate Club!" I heard this often as a child, this praise for having consumed every bite. I heard it often enough that I began to wonder more about this club of which I was a part. Did we, the Clean Plate Club members, do anything other than eat? Were there meetings I should be attending? Was someone going to send me a certificate or a badge signifying membership?

As I grew older and grappled with the disappointment that there was not, in fact, an actual club, the phrase took on a different tone. It stopped sounding like praise.

"Well, I can see *you're* definitely a member of the Clean Plate Club!" This would come from a relative, maybe someone I only saw a few times a year, as they expressed their shock at my ability to eat mass quantities of food.

My husband also grew up a member of the Clean Plate Club. With two older siblings and busy parents, his household formed a paranoia in him that there would not be enough to eat. He's prone to eating at unhealthy speeds, for which I sometimes kick him under the table. When I do this, he puts his fork down and looks up as if coming out of a stupor. He'll look around curiously. It's as if he blacks out while shoveling food into his mouth and needs to be brought back to consciousness.

When you put the two of us together, you have two people who do not excel at leaving food on the plate. We simply finish what is before us. We're just trying to be polite.

Years ago, we had an opportunity to attend a seven-course wine dinner at a restaurant of fine dining. I'd written a magazine article on the restaurateur. He'd been so pleased with my work[60] that he invited Mike and me to sit with him at the head table for the dinner, something that otherwise would have been well beyond our means.

We sat down at the table and were introduced to the others. We were fed things with fancy ingredients and words I couldn't pronounce, like fennel-brazed brie *en crut* with venison and raspberry coulis. We attempted to appear proper and as if we belonged there. My foot was poised and ready to kick Mike under the table if need be. I tried to leave a little bit of food on each plate, lest one of the other guests point out that I was obviously a member of the Clean Plate Club. It was difficult, because the food was so good and served in small portions, necessary when serving up seven courses.

The true challenge was the wine. Each place setting included three wine glasses, and each course was paired with three wines to taste along with the food. While my husband and I knew how to *drink* wine, we did not know how to merely *taste* it. This, coupled with the fact that staff stood rigidly behind us and immediately filled any glass that neared being empty, did not bode well.

It turns out that wine makes me loud. At one point, the restaurateur, who I'm sure grew more and more disenchanted with me as the evening progressed, stood to introduce the

---

[60] *After reading the article, he looked me in the eye and, with not the slightest attempt at disguising his shock, said, "Wow, you can actually write!"*

wine maker who was in attendance and who shared with us the history and complexities of each wine. She was elegant and sleek, long and lithe, and seemed to be draped in large swaths of fabric. The same outfit on me would have made me look like a taupe version of the Pillsbury doughboy, but on her it was European chic.

The restaurateur then announced that he'd be traveling to Spain to visit the vineyard the following year and that this organized wine trip was open to others for a mere $4,000 per couple. When he asked the room at large if anyone else would be attending, I loudly proclaimed, "We'll go!"

He looked at me, hesitant but also hopeful. Surely he questioned my ability to make such a statement, but he also seemed buoyed by the fact that he had a taker, as if he needed only one, and then the others would follow suit. "Okay," he said. "You'll attend?"

"No!" I laughed. The notion that Mike and I could afford a wine trip to Spain was hilarious. It made as much sense as the idea of us traveling to Mars for the weekend.

The restaurateur smiled weakly, attempting to be polite but no doubt annoyed, then repeated his inquiry.

"We're going to Spain!" I announced, unable to shut up.

`I thought I was being funny. In reality, I was loud and obnoxious.

We took a cab home that night, relieved the babysitter, and woke the next morning with splitting headaches, to the painful reality that babies and toddlers give no quarter to parents with hangovers.

* * *

Years later, trips to Spain *would* become a reality. We'd learn to use airline miles and home exchanges to make such trips affordable. We fell in love with the Basque region and at one point, during a trip when we were accompanied by Mike's parents, visited a cider house. Long, wooden tables crowded an expansive dining hall, which inexplicably brought to mind Vikings. The tables were set with silverware and bisected with spines of bread, giant baguettes placed carefully down the middle. The baguettes were sizable and sturdy enough to do battle with, or perhaps to provide needed carbohydrates to overindulgent cider enthusiasts. I gave our name, and a large, burly man (possibly a Viking) led us first to a stack of glasses. We each took one and followed him to our table. No one spoke English, but by watching others, we realized that we could take our glasses into an adjacent barrel room and fill up on as much cider as we wanted.

Only it's not quite that simple.

The cider is in massive barrels, wooden containers that reach the ceiling and occasionally have small taps a good five feet off the ground. When you turn on the tap, the cider streams in a thin line, creating a huge arc shooting 6 to 8 feet out to the middle of the floor (which has periodic drains in it for obvious reasons). Instead of filling your glass right at the tap, you hold your glass down by your knees out toward the end of the arc to provide a little added aeration, which makes a big difference in the taste, as Spanish ciders are typically still, not sparkling.

Pouring Spanish cider, also known as "throwing the cider," seemed like a great skill for my daughters to learn, as I was fairly certain it was absent from the curriculum at their elementary school. Europe is great for these unique teaching moments, where you can escape the American notion that children should be shielded from (and sometimes blatantly lied to about) anything having to do with alcohol. I was pretty sure that no one in that cider house was going to call Child Protective Services on us, so after watching the cider-pouring technique of others and demonstrating once ourselves, we let Emilia and Ivy hold the glasses.

"You ready?" Mike asked.

"Yes," Emilia said confidently. He turned on the tap, and Emilia held the glass low to catch the stream, as if every ten-year-old knows how to do such things. We repeated the process with Ivy. All of this was managed without once dousing our children in alcohol, which I think means that we are winning as parents.

"This is really good," said Ivy, "because I need to learn these things for when I'm a waitress someday." Ivy looked forward to a career as a waitress and from the age of three had been asking, "Can I be your service?" This meant she wanted to wait on someone. The day she tired of being my service was a sad one.

When the four adults had cider in hand, we took a sip. I'd been forewarned not to expect what passes for cider in America. Spanish cider is not only *not* sweet, it's downright sour. It's also been described as musty, having dominant wild yeast and notes of vinegar, leather, and farmyard. I'm not making this up. It actually makes sense when you consider the origins of the drink, especially in light of the particular cider house in which we found ourselves. The Petritegi estate was started five hundred years ago by a man who wanted his family, agricultural business, and livestock all housed in the same structure. Bring on the notes of farmyard.

That isn't to say cider goes back a mere five hundred years. The Northern Spanish dove headlong into heavy cider production in the eleventh century when they realized they'd have better luck cultivating apples than grapes. And cider's purpose didn't originate in getting overindulgent people like myself mildly buzzed. It was imperative, produced by Basques for ship crews, with three liters stored per day, per crewman. Because it was fermented, it could be stored longer and more safely than water. The eight-cups-a-day water consumption practice is fairly recent, if you consider it within the broader context of human history. Fermentation wasn't for frat parties; it was a dependable tool for hydration. Fermentation was *necessary*.

While I had a reasonable expectation of what Spanish cider would taste like, and was in no way disappointed by it, I hadn't shared this knowledge with my in-laws before they took their first sips. I could tell from the look on my mother-in-law's face that she thought we'd tapped a bad keg and was debating saying something, wondering who would acknowledge it first. My father-in-law's expression dropped.

"It's okay," I assured them. "That's what it's supposed to taste like."

"What's wrong, Papa?" Emilia asked her grandfather. "Don't you like it?"

He looked at her but said only, "Hmm."

"Well, that is definitely not what I was expecting," said my mother-in-law. She took another sip. "Maybe if I drink more of it, it will taste better."

"I think I'll wait for a glass of wine later," said my father-in-law.

Mike and I had no such qualms about drinking leathery

vinegar with notes of barn, as we returned many times to refill our glasses throughout our visit.

When we returned to our table, we found a waitress (who didn't look at all like a Viking). She'd brought a bottle of apple juice for the kids to share, and as she filled their cups, she spoke in rapid Spanish. All heads turned to me. I asked her to speak slowly and let her know that, regrettably, my feeble Spanish was all that was available at the table. It didn't come out that eloquently though, probably more like, "Speaking slow with please is my sorry my Spanish only they don't speak, yes?"

"Ah," she said in understanding, and then continued with more machine-gun Spanish. I sensed I was being asked to make a decision of some kind, because when I tried alternating between answers of *si* and *no*, in the hopes that it might be a yes-or-no question, this seemed unsatisfactory.

I changed tactics. "What recommend?"

She liked this and smiled before launching into more high-speed Spanish, this time accompanied by a fair amount of sign language, which either indicated many different plates or meant that we were about to be attacked by a fleet of round alien spaceships. It was fifty-fifty.

I smiled, nodded, and announced, *"Perfecto!"*

"So, what's happening?" my father-in-law asked when she left.

"I think she's going to bring us a little bit of each dish," I answered. I left out the possibility of aliens.

"Can I have some of the bread, Mom?" Emilia asked.

"Yes, go for it." I looked around for plates but saw none. In addition to the bread and glasses, our table was set with napkins and silverware, but no plates. Other patrons ate directly off the table, so we broke bread and did the same. Only later would I see that when literally breaking the bread, others would turn and hold the baguette over the floor. As a result, the floor of the cider house was covered with crumbs, but the tables were relatively clean, save for our table, where we approached it backwards. This would be common throughout our time in Spain. I'm conditioned to not drop crumbs or trash on the floor. In Spain, the floor was meant for such things.

The first course presented was two plates of sausage cut into small sections. I took a tentative bite. My husband and in-laws dove in.

"What do you think of this sausage?" I asked. "It kind of has an odd consistency."

"I think it's delicious," said my father-in-law.

"Yes," his wife concurred. "This is very good."

I looked to my husband, who nodded his agreement.

I'm squeamish with meat. An odd consistency makes me constantly question exactly which part of the animal I'm consuming (not that I really want to know), which does well to get in the way of *enjoying* the food. My consistency issues are confined to land animals. I have no problem consuming raw fish or swallowing oysters, and I am delighted by the slimiest of okra.

Instead of eating more sausage, I took my fair share of the giant baguettes and eagerly wondered what the next course would be. The waitress returned with the second course, setting down two plates of what *looked* like *tortilla de patata*, the traditional Spanish omelet of eggs and potatoes, which we'd all enjoyed on more than one occasion by that point in the trip. But as she placed the two omelets on the table, I heard the world *bacalhau*. I'd first encountered the Spanish word for cod while in Brazil (it's the same in Portuguese). These were cod omelets, a traditional food served in Spanish cider houses. It should be noted here that the aforementioned flavors of cider, which may not initially sound all that appealing, are meant to enhance the qualities of the food the cider is consumed with, cod omelet being one of those notable dishes.

The first bite was not bad.

The second bite was not good.

The third bite was confirmation that I had not consumed sufficient cider.

It wasn't just the combination of fish and runny eggs but also that it appeared the omelet was the vehicle for ridding the kitchen of fish that needed to go. When fish is no longer prime for consumption, I can think of many uses for it other than as food for humans. Like food for an animal that doesn't mind fish past its prime. Or bait for catching fresher fish. Or just a good old-fashioned contribution to the trash.

"That's, uh, that's really something," I said. I didn't want to trash-talk the cod omelet. What if it was just like the sausage? What if it was really excellent and I was just being the picky, judgmental, unadventurous eater that I sometimes am?

"It's not bad," said my father-in-law, who is known to consume eggs in any form, at any time, with any ingredient.

"I don't know," said Mike. "This fish might be a little… off." He barely missed a beat before adding, "Girls, do you want to try it?"

Ivy shook her head no. Emilia quickly occupied her mouth with a giant hunk of bread.

Because there were no individual plates, all six of us used our forks to share from the two plates placed in the center of the table. Each course was served in this manner. Mike, his mother, and I began slowly pushing the current course in the direction of my father-in-law, who was slowing down in his cod omelet consumption but still seemed happy to deal with our shares. After another few minutes, he put down his fork.

"It's not tasting all that great anymore," he said. "I think I'm about done with that."

At this point, the waitress walked by and glanced at our table. We all sat with our hands in our laps, and no one made a move for their silverware, but she walked away without clearing anything.

"Maybe she'll take it away when she comes back around," I suggested. "Should we get more cider?"

"I want to do it!" Ivy said.

"Me too!" said Emilia.

"I might have to have more cider after that," said Nana. If you'd placed a vinegar-soaked saddle on the table, we'd likely all have gnawed on it to rid ourselves of the taste of the cod omelet.

We refilled our glasses and returned to the table, where the omelets still sat.

"She passed by once," said my father-in-law.

"There she is again," added my mother-in-law. Again the waitress surveyed our plates and walked away. "I don't think she's going to bring us the next course until we finish this."

I was transported back to the elementary school cafeteria, seated at a long bench with food in front of me that I didn't want to eat. I also felt the pressure of knowing that I couldn't go out to recess until I did. (How can you have any pudding if you don't eat your meat?) Whether it's a cod omelet or an elementary school cafeteria hamburger, the dilemma is the same. On the one hand, you don't eat it because you don't want to eat it. On the other hand, if you will have to eat it eventually, you don't want to wait too long, because the colder a cod omelet or elementary school cafeteria hamburger gets, the greater its gross quotient.

"I'll do what I can," said my father-in-law. He took a deep breath, picked up his fork, and began working away at the two omelets. The rest of us felt a wave of gratitude.

"Thanks for taking one for the team, Dad," said Mike.

"But make sure you don't… hurt yourself," warned my mother-in-law, and I wondered what it would be like to sleep next to a spouse who, earlier in the day, had eaten massive amounts of eggs and questionable fish.

When he'd consumed more cod omelet than any human should ever have to, pushing the remaining pieces of fish and egg around on the plates to make it look like only bits were left as opposed to substantial chunks worth eating, the waitress mercifully returned.

"Are you finished?" she asked.

"Yes." I smiled my sweetest smile. "Thank you so much."

She took the plates away but looked a little confused by the fact that we hadn't licked them clean. She gave us a bit of a reprieve before bringing the next course.

"I wonder what it's going to be," I mused. "And how many more courses are coming."

"Can we go outside?" Emilia asked.

"Yes," said Mike, and the girls exited to play on the grounds of the *Sidrería* (or *Sagardotegia* in Basque).

The waitress returned, and before she even set down the two plates of the next course, I could see her mouth forming the word, her lips pressing together for that initial "b" in *bacalhau*.

More cod.

Thankfully, version two was a slightly fresher cod with peppers and onions, though I could tell in one more day this particular fish would have been relegated to an omelet. The peppers and onions that the fish came with were delightful.

The next course was different.

Because this time it was cod with *garlic*. And despite that I'd prayed I wouldn't be served more cod, version three was excellent, by far the freshest fish and skillfully prepared.

The meal was not yet over, and the final entree to arrive was a giant T-bone, delicious enough to overcome my skittish nature when it comes to meat. Our table descended upon the piece of meat with the voracity of me at a wine bar.

"Let's make sure the kids get a bite," I said. Turners are known to decimate feasts in shocking speeds. It's not that they're trying to be rude, but table manners aren't emphasized, and when in the presence of delicious food, instinct kicks in, and they resemble Tasmanian devils congregating over fresh roadkill. It's not pretty.

When the T-bone was at its end, my mother-in-law stared at it and said, "This is quite the hunk of bone. One could chew on that for a while." For just a second, I thought she was going to pick up the massive bone with her fingers and begin gnawing on it. And I thought, *Please don't.*

When the waitress came back around with one final plate, I had the irrational but terrifying thought that she was going to make us eat another cod omelet for dessert, but she instead presented us with fruit and cheese.

"I thought that was a blast," said my mother-in-law as we exited the dark dining hall into brilliant sunshine.

"I think I need to lie down," said my father-in-law.

"I really enjoyed that too," I said. "What did you think, Emilia?"

"The bread was delicious."

"When we get home, can I have a snack?" Ivy asked.

ö Ö ö

CHAPTER 21
CONSTELLATION PRIZE

My alcohol consumption has been fairly worldly over the years. In addition to consuming ciders in Spain, I've guzzled vodka in Russia, Caipirinhas in Brazil, ales in the UK, and sought out the infrequent but existing liquor stores in Morocco. I've sloshed my way through countless social occasions, sometimes with regrettable outcomes, and other times not. As my mid-forties rolled around, I embarked on a new adventure, the very idea of which strikes terror in many of my drinking friends… I went on hiatus from alcohol.

Like most people who break from drinking, I'd been thinking about it long before I actually took the plunge. Once I was honest with myself about the pros and cons of removing alcohol from my diet, I went all in. I didn't taper off or moderate; I just stopped consuming alcohol completely. This decision was followed by excitement. Think of all there is to gain! I'd lose weight, sleep better, have clearer skin and healthier hair and nails, and just think of how happy my liver and heart and all those important internal elements would be. Yay, me!

But sometimes the body is a dick. Maybe it has nothing to do with the timing of when I stopped drinking, but I experienced a fairly significant case of acne. On my ass.

Not a small patch, not one or two pimples, not limited to a single cheek. No, in my case, it was an impressive spread of large blemishes spanning the full width of my backside. The grouping almost resembled constellations, and I wondered if my butt wasn't somehow the recipient of messages sent from a distant planet that needed to be decoded using our knowledge of the night skies. I fully realize that this sounds like the worst movie script of all time, but it's exactly what went through my mind.

This seemed terribly unfair. I'd given up alcohol—this was a brave and healthy and noble decision. I had taken a stand for my own health and well-being, yet I was rewarded with a constellation of acne on my butt cheeks. Acne which, I might add, lasted for a solid two months.

Quitting drinking seems difficult at first, especially when it's become such a habit, when it seems like a friend with whom you sit and relax every evening.[61] Once you make the decision, though, you find it's much easier not to drink. All of the normal thoughts you don't realize you have as a drinker dissipate. There's no more mental energy spent on the logistics of drinking, like what to drink, what it will cost, when, how much, with whom, who will drive, and how to navigate a hangover should your alcohol consumption get to that level. Instead, you're free to do other things, productive things, healthy things, hobby-type things, and spend time on what really matters, like researching butt acne cream.

Many people who remove alcohol from their lives go on to do amazing things like run marathons and climb mountains. Part of this is because when you realize how much healthier you're becoming, that then begins to feed on itself. I have yet

---

61 *Or afternoon. Or midday. If you work from home and throw in a stressor like a pandemic, honestly time loses all meaning anyway.*

to run marathons or climb mountains. Instead, when I stopped drinking, I took up the pastime of Eating All the Things. This was in part to satiate the sugar cravings I experienced. And also because I was so pleased with myself, I felt I deserved a reward of some kind. Or many kinds. If you normally have two glasses of wine but then abstain, you feel entitled to order dessert. Or order dessert and then go home and raid your kids' candy jar and maybe buy a candy bar at the grocery store and then eat it in the car quickly so you can dispose of the wrapper so no one will know. These are the same things I did when I was pregnant, only this time I wasn't growing another human inside of me. I was just growing.

After a few months, I passed beyond the stage of Eating All the Things. The constellation prize on my ass faded, and for the first time in many years, I understood the feeling of truly getting a good night's sleep. I still have no plans to climb mountains or run marathons, but that's okay. There are other new experiences to navigate. One of which is uttering the (previously unthinkable) phrase: "I don't drink." Depending on the context, voicing the fact that you don't drink will either make you feel like a rock star or a leper.

The rock star instance usually happens in places where there's a focus on health, like the doctor's office. Someone is running you through a list of health questions, like "How have your bowels been functioning lately?" And, if you're female, a lot of small talk regarding your breasts and vagina. When they get around to the questions regarding your daily health habits, they'll come to one about alcohol consumption. In the past, this always presented itself to me in the form of a complex math problem. You take the truth of how many drinks you have per week, cut it in half, delete a few days for good measure, then throw the whole thing out and just blurt out what you think an acceptable answer might be. When you give up the sauce, you save yourself the mental calculations and instead go straight to, "I don't drink." Instant rock star status. At least in that doctor's office, in your mind, for that one particular moment.

The leper scenario is, unfortunately, far more common. This occurs everywhere in your life outside of the doctor's office. Or: anywhere you go where there are other adults present.

"Hey, how's it going?" They don't wait for an answer because the point is really what comes next. "We have beer, wine, cocktails. What would you like?"

"I'd love a water."

This is immediately met with stares of incredulity. If someone has known me well for any period of time within the past two decades, they might also exclaim, "Who *are* you?"

I don't fault people for this reaction. I used to do the same thing. When you drink, you can't imagine why anyone else would not drink, barring pregnancy or Mormonism. You also tend to assume that anyone who doesn't drink must have a *problem*. The truth is, once you stop, most of your problems go away. Except for the butt acne.

CHAPTER 22
HAPPY DAYS AND ZIP TIES

Mike had his eye on four electric bikes for our family for quite some time. To make himself feel better about the expense, he first sold his beloved mountain bike. It's not as if he had conquered any mountains in recent years, and one household needs only so many bikes, unless you're a crazy bike person in the way that I'm a crazy plant person. One household can never have too many plants, especially when you kill them at the rate that I do.

With the electric bikes, you can decide exactly how much work you want to do. And let's be honest: when most of us have the option, we'll choose less. Because of the assistance of a motor, our family of four can now ride from our house to downtown and back, even in extreme heat, without breaking a sweat.

Mike and I have always loved a small German bar downtown called Prost, even when I'm on hiatus from alcohol. I still enjoy going there. And thanks to a fancy bottled root beer, which I must concede is excellent as far as root beers go, our daughters love going there too. As a result, we take our daughters to the German bar fairly regularly. Sometimes that's enough of an outing, and sometimes we venture on to dinner at another restaurant before beginning the trek back home. Thanks to Boise's Greenbelt, a system of paved walking and biking paths that run the length of the city, most of our bike ride occurs along a picturesque route. As we ride underneath a canopy of trees and the air smells summer sweet, I know that my husband is in his happy place. In fact, he's admitted to me that when the four of us ride downtown, it's pretty much his ideal activity. I enjoy it also, though I feel that the monologues running through our brains along the ride are probably very different.

Mike: *What a great day! These bikes are awesome, and I'm so glad I have my little portable speaker with me so we can listen to music along the way. How cool is this, that all four of us can ride downtown together?*

Me: *What a great day! These bikes are awesome, and I bet that some demon kid, a future murderer, is lying in wait at the top of that grassy hill, looking at me through the scope of his BB gun right now. He's practicing for one day when he becomes a mass shooter. He'll probably shoot me in the neck, and I'll have a really gnarly crash because I'm going so fast. I hope they catch him. I hope they catch that fucker.*

Of course, there is no troubled youth aiming or shooting at me, and the outing occurs without a hitch. But this is what goes through my mind along the way. Because it could happen.

Both Emilia and Ivy enjoy these rides too. My only worry is that they'll stop enjoying these outings because of the corresponding safety lectures that go along with them. As soon as we arrive downtown and begin locking up the bikes, the lecture begins. Mike and I usually tag team the lecture delivery, though sometimes he just takes it and runs with it and there's no stopping him. The lecture will rehash previously discussed bike safety issues, and then we'll have to walk through everything that happened on the ride.

"Did everyone see that car that ran the red light? That's why this is important. You always stop and look."

"We know," the girls will say with a roll of the eyes. And they do know, but knowing that they know does nothing to dampen the fire of fear Mike and I have for their safety. Repeatedly lecturing them at least makes us feel like we're doing our part to keep them safe.

Hopefully their thought processes during the bike rides more resemble Mike's (*Yay! Happy day!*) than they do mine (*Who can spot the murderer?*). It could be that that's not the case. Every now and then, one of my daughters will tell me something they've been thinking with which I will immediately identify. For instance, they'll describe a plan of action they've devised with an elaborate self-defense system in place, and I'll know that they are undeniably my daughters.

I once received the following text message from Ivy:

Ivy: Mom?

She does this often, both in text and face-to-face conversation. I've tried to explain that she doesn't need this lead-in, that she's more than welcome to just launch into conversation with me at any time.

Me: Yes?

Ivy: When are you going to be home?

Me: Probably in a few minutes.

Ivy: Okay.

Ivy: Mom?

Me: Yes?

Ivy: Where's Dad?

Me: He's at home with you. He's downstairs, working.

Ivy: Oh. Good… Because I thought he was with you and then I heard someone in the house and right now I'm in your room, under your bed, and that's where I'm texting you from and I'm kind of stuck under here.

She'd wriggled her way out from under the bed by the time I got home. What I learned from that exchange is that we're probably good on lectures about things like bike safety but definitely need to work on our Intruder Response Plan. Because she 100 percent failed. I had obviously not given my eleven-year-old daughter enough true crime case studies.

1. If you have your phone, go ahead and skip me in your decision tree of who to call and jump straight to the police.

2. When you do call the police, you don't need to work up to the conversation slowly by first saying, "Hello? Police?" and waiting for them to say, "Yes." Just get right to the point.

3. If you're hiding from a potential intruder, but doing it right next to one of the home's exits, just go ahead and take that exit. Don't wait to see if the intruder is

smart enough to look under the bed.

When I was her age, I had all sorts of contingency plans for such scenarios. I'd keep things like a lighter and can of Aqua Net nearby, so that if needed, I could fashion a blow torch and aim it at my intruder's face. I knew which decorative objects had the most heft to them and therefore might be effective in delivering a blow to the head. And when I was a kid, zip ties were not the ubiquitous little tools they are now, but if I'd known about them then, I'd have kept a few in my pocket at all times, in case I needed to secure my assailant until the authorities arrived. The authorities would of course be police officers who would arrest the bad guy, commend me for my quick thinking and heroic actions, and offer me a spot on the force, straight to detective. There would also be EMTs on the scene to address the intruder's wounds, which at this point would include facial burns where I'd sprayed him with flaming Aqua Net, head trauma where I'd beaned him on the noggin with a nearby sculpture, and lacerations around the wrists, procured when he struggled futilely against my zip tie restraints. He'd also need a bag of frozen peas for his groin, because chances are I'd have given him a few kicks to that area while waiting for police to arrive, just because that's what that fucker deserved.

I know there's an alternate possibility in this type of scenario, one in which I completely freeze up into a whimpering pile of tears and urine, but I like the first scenario better.

ö Ö ö

CHAPTER 23
ON VANITY

Vanity is a powerful force. As I make my way through my forties into the latter half of life, I find that I'm more prone to vain practices, the same ones I eschewed when I was younger. I'm as much a sucker for an overpriced and ineffective eye cream as anyone. Pre-pandemic, I gave into vanity and decided I would have my teeth straightened. They weren't entirely out of sorts but had shifted enough since my teenage bout of braces to begin bothering me when I looked in the mirror. In the beginning, I just wanted one of my front teeth filed down so that it was more in line with its neighbor. When I asked my dentist about it, he said that I might be better served by seeing an orthodontist. Because the problem wasn't so much that one tooth was too long, but that the other one was trying to retreat up into my gums.

When I first walked into the orthodontist's office, I found myself in the waiting room with half a dozen teenagers. Twice, I was asked by a receptionist what my child's name was.

"Well, I have two kids, but they're not here," I explained. "I'm actually the patient."

Both times, she looked apologetic and made a great show of letting me know that they serve women of my age all the time (just never when I happened to have an appointment).

I used Invisalign for a solid year, getting all my teeth to do what they are supposed to do, except for the pesky tooth

I'd been out to fix in the first place. It simply refused to cooperate. On a visit that was supposed to be one of my last, the orthodontist said, "You know, we can keep trying this, or you can just let me slap some braces on there. It will fix it in no time. You'll probably only need them on for a few weeks."

I'd endured braces for four years in my youth, an experience I was sure I'd never have to go through again. But there I was, mid-forties, getting braces on my teeth. It would only be for a short time, I told myself.

A week after that appointment, with a mouth newly minted with metal, the coronavirus reached full bloom in the United States and my orthodontist's office shut down for six months. I had metal in my mouth, but I couldn't have my braces adjusted during that time, so they served no purpose, other than sustaining a higher level of awkwardness than my standard fare. Only once did I contemplate getting a pair of pliers to bend the wires in what I thought might be the right directions. I didn't, though, because I didn't want to relate the whole stupid story to an ER doctor when asked how I managed to remove my own teeth with a pair of pliers.

Eventually, the office reopened and the orthodontist was able to adjust my braces to make sure they served their intended purpose. And then they were removed, and I was given a retainer, and with perfect teeth I could put the whole experience behind me.

Until that single traitor incisor again began attempting to retreat upwards. What if it was a secret alien implant that wanted to journey not only into my upper gumline but then further make its way north into my brain? Obviously, I couldn't let that happen, so I returned to the orthodontist, who tried a variety of MacGyver-worthy fixes until finally, again, conceding that the best course of action would be to wear braces for a few months.

"And this time," he assured me, "once they're in place, I'll put a permanent retainer [62] on the back of your teeth so it doesn't happen again." I didn't really know what that meant, but I said okay.

Strangers don't feel the need to comment on an adult's braces, but friends and family sure do. Most of the time, before they voice an inquiry, they look at me and pull their own lips back, baring their perfect teeth, as an unspoken acknowledgment that they're about to launch into a discussion about my *im*perfect teeth.

"Yes," I have to say. "I have braces again."

They usually follow this up with "Why?"

As if I might be doing it just for fun. Or as an accessory. Maybe I like the feel of having the inside of my mouth torn up. Maybe I enjoy finishing a meal and then not knowing what horrors, in the form of food particles, are lurking within my face metal. Can there really be any appropriate response to why one might have braces other than "To straighten my teeth"?

During the saga of my orthodontist appointments, one of the technicians who worked on me got pregnant and had a baby. And yet my first ever pair of braces occurred long before that technician was ever born. It was as if my orthodontia was destined to span multiple generations. The tech was going to name her baby Hank, which made me smile a bit as she tweaked the wires that spanned my jaw. Maybe Hank would

---

62 *Basically, this is a wire glued to the back of my upper teeth. It's there 24/7, doing its job while remaining out of sight.*

be blessed with perfect teeth. And if not, surely his mother could sort him out.

Aside from eye cream and orthodontia, other pursuits of vanity include having age spots removed from my face with lasers. This sounds extreme until you have an age spot pop up on your face, at which point you begin looking around for the nearest laser with which to zap that sucker off. The skin, unless appropriately protected and babied, will be relentless with its backlash. At some point, it just doesn't want to play nice anymore, like it feels taken for granted in all the previous decades and now refuses to cooperate.

When it comes to combatting aging skin, I'm not yet ready to venture into the territory of injecting something *into* my face. I'll bankrupt myself with topical solutions and let those lasers fly, but I'm not emotionally ready at this point to go any step beyond that. This is in no way a suggestion that those treatments don't work. I know that they do.

I recently found myself in conversation with a woman who peppered our exchange with comments about how old she was, and about how much older than *me* she was. She felt the need to continually remind me of this, as if she had some sort of failing justified by the fact that she was *so much older* than me. Though she had no failings, at least not any that she was willing to admit to in conversation. And every time she'd remind me, "But that's just me because I'm *so old*, because I'm *so much older* than you…" I'd look at her perfectly youthful eyes. Without wrinkles, without bags. The skin under her eyes didn't look like mine, a stack of mini double chins always threatening to form. The really sucky thing about the type of eye age that I have is that smiling only makes it worse. Even a slight nod of appreciation at a mediocre knock-knock joke is enough to make my eyes add another twelve years to my age. Not ten, but *twelve*. I know this, because I've practiced different expressions in the mirror to see how my eyes contribute to my overall face under certain conditions. Smiling definitely makes it worse. The only expression I can adopt that makes my eyes look not quite so old is a wide-eyed look of surprise, with an accent of stupidity thrown in. It's true. Look in the mirror with wide eyes, as if you've just discovered an unsourced pile of vomit in the middle of your living room, then add in a layer of slight stupidity over this, and your eyes will take on a more youthful countenance. Or, like me, say screw it and prefer to be old and smiley. At least my teeth look good.

CHAPTER 24
I LOVE YOU, BUT I'M ALLERGIC TO YOU

When the pandemic hit, I couldn't believe how many people went out and got pandemic puppies. *Suckers!* I thought. Until we got one ourselves. We'd strictly been a no-pets household up until the flock of chickens, with the exception of a few hermit crabs, which I cared for until they died peacefully in their sleep of natural causes.[63]

Our puppy wasn't so much the result of the pandemic, but more the result of a successful campaign by Ivy to guilt us into dog ownership. It's ironic, given that when Ivy was small, dogs terrified her. We once attended a dinner at the home of some friends, and Ivy snuck out of the house and huddled down in the back seat of the car for half an hour after catching sight of a dog crate. She didn't see the actual animal, as our friends knew of her fear and had the dog sequestered upstairs in their bedroom. The crate alone was enough to send her into a state of panic, and I was troubled not only by her reaction, but also the fact that it was at least half an hour before we, her parents, noticed that she was missing.

Fast-forward a few years, and Ivy's greatest desire was to have a dog, or for us to have a family dog. It's important that we make that distinction because we all know that when Ivy strikes out on her own, I will still be the one walking the

---

63 *An assumption, yes, and how I choose to think of their demise.*

animal and scooping its poop.

Mike and I had owned dogs years ago, and after a series of unfortunate outcomes had sworn never to do so again. But Mike is, at heart, a lover of Labradors. And I cannot deny my urge to care for other living things. This extends beyond dogs and children, of course. If I could, I'd have a hundred chickens. And a pig. And every trip to the grocery store brings with it the temptation to buy another houseplant. I excel at justifying $18 spent on a plant that may or may not live another week:

- It cleans the air.
- It comes in a cute pot.
- It makes me happy.
- Sometimes I'm tempted to select groceries online and have them delivered. This would come with a delivery fee of ten dollars. With all of the money I'm saving by picking up my own groceries, surely I deserve another plant.

My biggest fear about renewing my membership in the Society of Crazy Dog People was allergies. Both my children have allergic reactions to some dogs, but not all. This wasn't enough of a concern for us to seek out a hypoallergenic breed. To get Mike on board with the dog idea, it would have to be a Labrador and only a Labrador. Not a labradoodle or golden-labra-schnauzer-doodle or some such other creature. But what if the girls were allergic? I decided not to give the matter too much thought. We'd keep the dog out of their bedrooms and simply drug our children if necessary. Because that's what Crazy Dog People do.

When Mike and I picked up our new pet, she was

everything we hoped for—a happy, mushy ball of puppy. We did this in secret and had farmed our kids out to a friend's house the day before, so that they'd return that afternoon to find the puppy. When they did so, I was ready with my camera to capture the shock and tears. As predicted, Ivy broke down, and it was glorious.

There was the issue of naming the dog, something that proved difficult. I wanted to name her Rabbit or Ninja and was staunchly against anything like Cocoa or Fluffy. The dog was a silver Lab, which is apparently a thing. I'd thought that Labs came in only three varieties—yellow, chocolate, or black—but when Mike went looking for one, he stumbled upon silver. I believe they're called silver Labs because that sounds better than "taupe" or "brownish."

We never did fully agree on a name, but we got close. Everyone liked a variation of June, so depending on whom you ask, her name is Juno/Juneau, Juniper, June Bug, or June Osbourne.[64]

It turns out that the kids had no allergies whatsoever. Unfortunately, my sinuses revolted entirely. I popped allergy pills as if they were Tic Tacs. For weeks, my eyes were puffy and red,[65] and I didn't move from one room to the next without first making sure I had a full box of tissues at the ready. At no point did I consider getting rid of the dog. I was allergic to her, yes. But I loved her more.

In addition to a combination of prescription and over-the-counter medications to get me through my allergy

---

64 *If you're not familiar, this is a nod to* The Handmaid's Tale.

65 *More so than normal. No amount of eye cream could combat this level of inflammation.*

(it subsided—or my body adapted—as she made the transition from puppy to dog), I used a neti pot. If you've never used a neti pot, it looks like a small teapot, and you fill it with a warm saline solution. You then pour the warm salt water into your nose. It's like the ocean, only you get salt water up your nose on purpose. Not only up your nose, but you cock your head in a manner so that the water travels up one nostril and through your nasal passage until it comes out the other nostril. I like to think of it as an enema for your face.

When it comes to face enemas, you have to wonder who first came up with the idea. Stricken with an unusually brutal cold, someone suddenly thought, *Ooh, I know! I'm going to pour warm salt water up my nose. That'll make me feel better!* Likewise, with enemas of the traditional variety. How did that first one go down? Was there a hose of some sort involved? Were there early difficulties in regulating pressure? I have so many questions and yet I'm fearful of knowing the answers.

Puppies are floppy and mushy and cute, but also mouthy. They're compelled to get those sharp little puppy teeth on anything they can, including human flesh. Because I was the family member who spent the most time with June, my right arm in those early weeks was in a constant state of injury. That's okay though. I'll take a scratched-up arm over a crotch bite any day. And dogs will do that, randomly bite your crotch and wonder why you get all pissed off about it. They must think we're terribly uptight, which is also why they must love playing with other dogs so much. I imagine they think, *Finally, someone who* gets *me*, because when two Labradors are together, particularly puppies, anything goes. There is an explicit agreement that all bets are off, that sniffing, licking, biting, and pawing of any area is not only tolerated but encouraged.

Dog ownership means you will end up Googling things that otherwise never would have occurred to you to ask:

- How many slugs is it safe for a dog to eat?
- Why does my female dog like to hump her blankie?
- Is my dog chewing through my phone cord in an attempt to reduce my screen time or is she just being an asshole?

Of the many ways to deter a dog from chewing on something, the simplest and most effective method is to simply make the object in question inaccessible to the dog. This becomes more difficult when your dog enjoys chewing on something like, for example, the walls of your home.

On more than one occasion, June has widened her jaws as much as possible and maneuvered her head to a side angle so that she can graze her teeth along a flat wall. What perplexes me is that she'll engage in this behavior while surrounded by a plethora of chew toys. Not just your Dollar Store variety chew toys, but also a selection from our local foo-foo pet store that exists for owners of dogs with names like Fifi.[66]

You can learn a lot of things at a foo-foo pet store just by browsing the aisles, especially if a decade has passed since the last time you were a dog owner. It's a lot like the changes in parenting. In what my daughters call "the olden days," or pre-1985, you might have taken your baby home from the hospital in a shoebox. Now they use these things called car

---

[66] *Apparently, it also exists for me, because as much as I ridicule the store, I also spend a small fortune there.*

seats. It's similar with dogs. At a foo-foo pet store, you learn that rawhide, once a staple, is now viewed in the same light as parents view lead paint. As in, it's not good. As such, you can purchase a variety of dog treats that are rawhide-free rawhides. These same items are purported to last your dog a solid hour of chew time, which means most animals will consume them in two to three minutes.

I now know that rawhide is bad—unless you buy the rawhide-free rawhide. And leashes are bad, of course, because no one wants to be yanked around by the neck. Harnesses are preferred. I get this, as personally I'd much rather be yanked around by my armpits.[67] It's basic logic.

Other items in the foo-foo pet store leave me confounded. For instance, you might look at the ingredients of a dog treat out of curiosity and find that it includes both pork platelets and organic rosemary extract. I'd always assumed that when it came to meat in dog food and treats, even the expensive, foo-foo variety, these were scraps from the floor of a meat-processing plant. Apparently, there is a much more discerning process, one that involves specifically harvesting the pork *platelets*. And these platelets obviously pair nicely with organic rosemary extract. Either that or the manufacturers of these dog treats guessed that people who shop for overpriced dog treats want to see items in the ingredients list like pork platelets and organic rosemary extract.

I happen to have a giant, unruly rosemary bush in my garden. I'm thinking I could save some money by chopping off a sprig and offering it to my dog to chew on, because what she'll get out of it will undoubtedly be organic

_____
67 *After all, I do aerial yoga.*

rosemary extract. Sadly, I'm fresh out of pork platelets.

Like most pet owners, I now occasionally find myself in a state of paralysis. I can't move, lest I sacrifice the comfort of this animal. Sure, she wanted to gnaw my face off a minute ago, and yes, she wouldn't hesitate to vomit into my cleavage if she felt so inclined, but now she's sleepy and has her cute little head resting on my lap, so I'll sit here with limbs unnaturally contorted and going numb so I don't disturb her.

Eventually, we had to come up with a plan for how the dog would be cared for when we travel. Obviously, this is something that can be figured out. I know plenty of dog owners who are not shackled to their homes because of pet ownership, and fear of that shackling was one thing that kept us from having pets for so long.[68] We could have pet sitters and house sitters and chicken sitters, or we could board the dog.

When our first trip came, it was two and a half weeks in Mexico to host a series of retreats, something that had been in the works for the previous year and a half. Our first possibility was to put June in the care of Mike's brother, Virgil, who'd been longing for a dog for quite some time. For a variety of reasons that would constitute another book, Virgil is unable to take on a dog of his own, so him having our dog for a short period of time seemed ideal. He could get his canine fix, and June would be taken care of in our absence. As the trip inched closer, however, we realized this was not a viable plan. Virgil's day-to-day life didn't have room for a dog, even on a short-term basis, and the amount of attention that a puppy needed was too much of a favor to ask in any case. What if she ate

---

[68] *The hermit crabs never seemed to mind when we traveled. Or if they did, they never mentioned it. At least not to me.*

his walls or randomly bit his crotch?

Virgil had bigger things to worry about. Chief among them, at least in my mind, was that he didn't have a functional shower. This meant he would occasionally show up at our house to shower, which invariably came with an update on other aspects of his life, like his need for massive quantities of baby powder to keep his testicles from chafing. I love Virgil, I really do, but I have endured more conversations about his chafed balls over the last twenty years than any human being should have to suffer.

With Virgil out of the picture as an option, Mike began researching boarding facilities, which quickly led to the discovery of boarding *and training* facilities.

"Not only do they board your dog," he explained, "but they also train it. And I found one an hour away that's only six hundred dollars for a whole month. They specialize in Labradors and have a huge property with ponds and everything."

"That sounds perfect," I agreed. "It's like she'll be going to summer camp for dogs."

From that moment on, I had the picture cemented in my mind. June was going to have so much fun. She'd get to play with other Labradors, go swimming, and come back to us trained and obedient. What was not to love?

I told our daughters and anyone who would listen how we'd discovered this most perfect of solutions. I was happy for June, excited on her behalf.

Until the day we dropped her off.

"Oh, look, they have chickens too," I said, noting a small coop as we pulled onto a dry scratch of land. A dozen dogs barked furiously, lined up in a row of kennels, an organized chaos of chain-link fence, concrete, and canine. As soon as we exited the truck, June tucked her tail between her legs and scurried to hide behind us. She loved other dogs, but this was overwhelming. *It's fine*, I told myself. *Of course they have kennels. What did you think, Amanda, that the dogs would get to curl up and snuggle together on a giant, fluffy dog bed?*

That's exactly what I'd thought, or at least hoped for. I'd have settled for a patch of grass. The woman who ran the operation greeted us, and I had no red flags waving in my mind based on our interaction. We briefly encountered two assistants she had milling around, a man so thin he looked like a walking bag of bones and a woman with telltale sores around her mouth that likely weren't the result of a mild case of herpes. Hallmarks of addiction aside, the people seemed nice and attentive to the animals.

Then the owner lady asked the mouth sores lady to get a pigeon so we could see how our dog would do. Over the next half hour, the horror of the situation descended upon me, including the fact that the structure I'd taken for a chicken coop was actually a halfway house for ill-fated birds.

The pigeon was a beautiful bird, dark gray feathers accented with iridescent purple when in the sun. This bird could have been a pigeon model, if such things exist. Its wings must have been clipped, because it couldn't fly away, though by all other accounts it was a healthy bird. Until the owner began throwing the bird a few feet away and then encouraging our dog to go get it.

"See how she's putting her mouth on the bird?" she asked us. "That's a great sign. I think she's going to do really great."

Really great as a hunting dog was what she meant. Her specialty was not simply in obedience training, and forget whatever fantasies I'd harbored about June frolicking at the water's edge with other Labs. This was where dogs went to be trained to hunt. Suddenly I remembered overhearing Mike's conversations on the phone when arranging June's stay. "Yeah, I don't really hunt a lot," he'd said. In fact, he doesn't hunt at all. He has hunted, having been born and raised in Alaska, but he's never been an avid hunter or necessarily enjoyed it.

"It's like fishing," he'll say. "Some guys just love it. Sure, I'll do it if it means I'm filling the freezer, but that's about it."

Aside from the fact that Mike doesn't hunt, the last thing I wanted our dog to learn was to stalk anything feathered. I love my chickens. Not as meals but as real live animals that I care for and which lay eggs.

The owner continued to chuck the pigeon and encourage June to go after it. The bird flopped around. In minutes, it had gone from a bird that could have graced the cover of *Modern Pigeon* to a bedraggled, slobbered on, barely alive creature with patches of missing feathers. It was cruel and grotesque.

I tried to voice the fact that I was most interested in obedience training, but I could see that the woman was truly in her element. She mentioned something about how our deposit money went to the procuring of live birds for training purposes, and I considered offering her money *not* to buy any more live birds. Eventually, she handed the now half-pigeon back to Mouth Sores.

"I'm not sure if that one's going to make it," she said.

I had a brilliant thought. I could take the bird. If they thought it would die anyway, I would take the bird and nurse it back to health and dote on it every day for the rest of its miserable, unfortunate life. And while I was at it, I'd take my dog home too, and she'd sleep on her nice, fluffy dog bed in our nice, air-conditioned house, the walls of which I'd discourage her from eating. We wouldn't put her in the concrete kennel, and we'd pretend this place never even existed.

But in thirty-six hours, we were getting on a plane. The pigeon would die for no good reason, June was shoved in her kennel against her will, and I cried during the drive back to Boise.

June was supposed to stay and work on retrieving dead birds for long after our Mexico trip, but I couldn't stand the idea of her being there any longer than necessary, and Mike wasn't far behind me. What sealed the deal was when we saw the forecast for the week after our return. Six consecutive days with high temperatures of 108 convinced us that we needed to bring June back to her cushy life asap.

When we brought her home from Bird Torture Camp, June was no more obedient than before. That's okay, though, because neither did she come home with a bloodlust for birds. She much prefers the taste of drywall.

CHAPTER 25
WASTE NOT

Having a dog comes with the opportunity to confront, multiple times a day, the issue of how much waste a living being can produce and what should be done with that waste. Before we got the dog, Mike acquired an array of fecal-scooping devices. I figured you really only need one, unless we're all going to be out there scooping poop together, like a fun family activity on a Saturday afternoon. I pictured our own version of a work-release program, where instead of doing time for our petty crimes, we go out and clean up the highway, or in our case, the backyard.

There's a scooper that comes down like the apparatus in the claw game, and you control the jaws that close around the offending poo to remove it. Then there's the rake and pan combo, which makes you look more like an affable janitor out cleaning up scraps of paper from the elementary school hallway, except it's dog shit from your own backyard. And of course one can always rely on the doggie bag method, especially when on the go. I always travel now with a clean roll of doggie bags in my purse, which may come in handy for other uses. The bags require more intimate contact with the poo, as you don't have a handle length between it and you, and no matter how hard you try, you will feel the texture of the matter.

No matter what you use to scoop or otherwise remove the

poo, it's always best when in solid form, which makes me want to occasionally slip my dog an Imodium for good measure, but I'm pretty sure that's not included in the Handbook of Good Dog Ownership.

Also, I hate the phrase doggie bag, because it makes me think of food so good that you have to take the leftovers home, which is definitely not how I think of dog shit. None of these solve the problem of what to do with all this poo, which eventually ends up in the landfill.[69]

I'm sure I'm not alone, or maybe I am, in experiencing thoughts that then lead to my own waste production. As a human being, I can't help but feel that's my legacy: all the things that I've broken and the waste I've left behind. At least I don't have to scoop my own poo, and instead, with the flush of a toilet, it is out of sight and out of mind.

With all the waste that people produce, we can ask ourselves the question of how we might produce less waste, but you can't really do that when it comes to poop. No one should poop less; that's not a viable plan for helping to save the planet. We can, however, use less toilet paper, something we've always known but weren't fully confronted with until the great toilet paper shortage of 2020, which accompanied the great pandemic of 2020.

I'd long been aware of the fact that many other countries are far ahead of us in this and other matters. Why are Americans so scared of bidets? We embrace NASCAR and bungee jumping and methamphetamine use, which are all far

---

[69] *Mike has since installed a doggy composting pit in the corner of our yard, but I need to make it through a full summer of this contraption before passing judgment on it.*

more dangerous. Why the fear of bidets?

Instead of answering this question, I ordered one. Spending $35 to be better to the environment and more hygienic in my nether regions seems like a win-win. Until I owned one, I had no idea that bidets come with such a variety of settings, and I ordered a cheap model. One of the settings is aimed, literally, at a woman's lady parts. Genius. Don't have time to shower? No problem. Just slap on some deodorant, wash your nether regions, and you're good to go.[70] Theoretically, I'm all in.

Practically, however, I still have some refining to do. What if I'm not correctly situated? Do I run the risk of using a forceful stream of water to shoot poo into my own vagina? Because that's not what I want at all. In fact, that's the opposite of hygienic.[71] I'm sure in time I'll have the bidet situation all sorted. I promise not to tell you about it.

* * *

When we visit some friends in the neighborhood, we always take our dog, because our dog has become good friends with their dog. To be fair, I think both dogs would consider themselves "good friends" with any other living creature that displays a willingness to play. When the two

---

[70] *Incidentally, the poo setting for the bidet shows a small outline of buttocks, but the lady parts setting shows an outline of a dress. I'd have found it far more entertaining if they'd had an artist's rendition of a vagina.*

[71] *Also, if you purchase and install a bidet, do not, out of curiosity, turn the bidet on without being seated on the toilet. You will only succeed in shooting a forceful stream of water at the opposing wall. No good will come of this.*

dogs greet each other, there is no initial hesitancy. They don't even pause to sniff one another's assholes. Instead, they immediately launch into combat. If they could talk, I imagine their dialogue would go something like this:

> **Bernie:** I'm going to try to bite your face off. Or do you want to try to bite my face off? Or we could go at the same time.

> **June:** That's a great idea. Let's face bite for a bit, and then maybe later we can sniff each other's assholes.

Then the face biting commences, which must be great fun, because it can go on for a full hour.

> **Bernie:** Hey, do you want to take a break for a minute? Do you want some water?

> **June:** Yeah. Does it have random things floating in it? Because that's my favorite kind of water.

> **Bernie:** Yes. I also drooled in it and stepped in it to make it extra good.

Drinking water of questionable hygiene commences.

> **Bernie:** Oh, hey, come over here. I want to show you something really cool.

> **June:** Okay, let me just chew on your face again for a second.

At this point, Bernie leads June to a kiddie pool that's

been set up just for him, to keep him cool during the summer months. Or maybe at one point the kiddie pool was set up for our friends' kids, but since Bernie has entered the picture, it has become his.

Bernie: Check out this water bowl. It's big and super awesome. It actually does three things at the same time. You can stand in it.

Bernie stands in the water.

Bernie: You can drink it.

Bernie drinks the water.

Bernie: And you can pee in it.

Bernie pees in the water.

June: So cool!

June stands in the water and drinks it while Bernie continues to pee.

Later they'll resume face biting, asshole sniffing, and spend the afternoon having diarrhea together.

We can look at the behavior of dogs and think they're gross (because they're gross), or we can observe them and realize just how uptight we humans have become. Don't get me wrong. I have no inclination to sniff anyone's asshole or drink from a kiddie pool of questionable water-to-urine ratio, but it seems we've also gone too far in the other direction... sometimes. Think about it: on the one hand, we're overly sanitized; on the other hand, we do disgusting things in the world of meat processing and packing, which lead to illnesses, which necessitate further sanitization. Did the dinosaurs experience similar dilemmas before biting the archaeological dust? Or was the problem more of a design flaw, like T-Rex's inability to reach the hand sanitizer even if it was right there in front of him?

Because June doesn't waste time contemplating such things and instead spends her time searching the dog park for goose poop to consume and drinking Bernie's pee, she had consistent diarrhea when our next trip rolled around.

After our disastrous experience with Bird Torture Camp, we settled on a doggie resort for future boarding, which is exactly what it sounds like. Instead of being outside in a kennel made of concrete and fencing in hundred-degree weather, she'd be inside on a softer floor made of a rubber composite, still with fencing, but this time with air-conditioning.

When you get a dog, you forget about the logic that animals survive in nature because they were originally part of nature before we adopted them and made them soft. You come to believe that your animal needs just as much comfort as you do. Even though humans should also be able to survive in nature instead of climate-controlled boxes.

Not only would June enjoy the comfort of air-conditioning, but she'd also get to play in the doggie play yard with other dogs. There would be ample opportunity for the dogs to chew on one another's faces.

We could not, however, send her to the doggie resort with diarrhea. That's akin to sending your child to school with pink eye or lice. It's a dick move. To cure her intestinal distress, I cooked chicken and rice and pumpkin. I supervised her consumption of random foreign objects. (I slipped her Imodium.) Her system thankfully righted itself. We were able to take our trip, June luxuriated at her doggie resort, and no pigeons were harmed in the process.

CHAPTER 26
I JUST REALIZED I'LL NEVER BE COOL

Maybe cool is overrated. Cool is the façade other people have perfected, but it could be that inside they're just as unsure and anxious as I am. Maybe the cool people are pretending to be The Fonz, but really they're all short little guys with names like Henry Winkler.

Cool people simply fail to admit things about which the rest of us are more forthcoming. Maybe I'm *too* forthcoming, but I'm willing to accept that. If I was cool, I'd probably keep the following information to myself. I am unsettled by:

- Toilets flushing while I'm still sitting on them.
- Foods that include the words loin, finger, belly, or cheek.
- When fish tastes fishy and the fact that I eat it anyway.
- When mangoes taste fishy and the fact that I eat them anyway.
- The number of people who don't even pretend to wash their hands after using a restroom, public or private.

My shower is a clear and undeniable indicator of the fact that I'll never be cool. While I imagine most women have beauty products made from things like hibiscus and lavender and lemongrass, mine come from charcoal and tar. I have to keep the bottles separate because they look so alike. There's the charcoal face wash to keep acne at bay and then the coal tar shampoo to calm my flaky head.

Every now and then, Emilia will give me a fancy bath product. It's not as if she's spending her money on a gift for me; rather, she's under the false impression that lotions and potions go bad over time. Once they're old, she doesn't want them anymore, thinking them no longer good (but apparently still good enough for me). I haven't dispelled this belief, because I'm able to benefit from it.

"Here, Mom. Do you want this?" she'll say, handing me a tub of coconut sugar scrub. "It's really old."

I guess I can understand her thinking. She knows that food goes bad over time, so it's logical to her that products claiming to be made from ingredients that are also foods would deteriorate in a similar manner. And just as I am the human garbage disposal when it comes to eating foods no one else wants, I have also become the recipient for unwanted toiletries. In this way, I've learned to buy her the gifts that I eventually want to inherit.

When I use a coconut sugar scrub, I admittedly smell better. I'm no longer what smells bad. If I were a dessert, and you take into account my other beauty products, I imagine myself to be a coconut-encrusted lump of coal. That about sums me up.

I've accepted the fact that I'll never be cool and now feel it is my job to preserve any chance my children might have of being cool. It's a sick, unhealthy version of wanting a better life for your children. I've failed at this in the past, like when I took them shoe shopping once. We returned with pink sparkly Trolls shoes for Ivy and all-black orthopedic sneakers for Emilia. Ivy was really into trolls at the time, and Emilia has feet that make her difficult to shop for. Only when we got home and showed Mike was I able to see the error of my actions through his eyes. He took one look at the shoes, then looked at me and plainly asked, "Do you want them to be bullied?"

Then there was the time Emilia wanted short hair, really short hair, and I let her. I've never stressed about hair length, style, or color. It's not like she wanted a tattoo at the age of ten. Hair grows. And everyone must go through and learn from the experience of getting a bad haircut at least once in their life. So I took the girls to the mall for haircuts, which was perhaps already setting us up for disaster. I allowed Emilia full freedom in telling the "stylist" how she wanted her hair cut. She held her hand up to her ear and said, "Short!" Many girls can pull off this type of haircut, but since Emilia is my daughter, she is not one of them. I let it happen, though, and before we left the "salon," she was in tears.

"Why would you let her do that?" Mike demanded. I wanted to bring up the "At least it's not a tattoo" defense, but quickly conceded that there would be no getting through to him because there really wasn't any light for him to see. I'd failed her. I'd allowed her to fully explore the depths of my own awkwardness. In the end, I offered to buy her a series of hats and scarves, but none of it really helped. Since then, I've tried to do better. I've tried to save them from me and save them from themselves. For instance:

"I won't take you anywhere until you put on a bra."

"Yellow plastic shower shoes are not appropriate to wear to a restaurant."

"No, the addition of socks does not improve the yellow plastic shower shoes."

Maybe I haven't made any headway at all, because I'm the one who allowed the purchase of the yellow plastic shower shoes in the first place. To be fair, the girls were headed to camp, where they'd be living in a dorm and were supposed to have shoes appropriate for wearing to the dorm shower, so that's exactly what I got them. The problem was that they wanted to continue wearing them to other places, meaning anywhere in public. When packing for the aforementioned camp, I did make sure my daughter's feminine products were not in the clear, exterior pocket of the backpack where Emilia had first placed them. The last thing you need to do is show up to camp and, before uttering your first hello, proclaim that you'll soon be having your period. Then again, I'm sure there are plenty of people who lead off with that very information. Maybe it helps them find their people.

To attend this camp, my daughters were allowed to travel on their own, navigating airports and gate changes. That's exciting and brave and, to be honest, pretty cool.

I'm getting better at staving off severe levels of embarrassment for my kids. For instance, if we're all in a public place and one of my daughters passes gas, I will loudly announce, "Excuse me!" I'll be the fall guy. I'm your huckleberry. Because lord knows it really is me most of the time anyway.

Sometimes I think Mike is cool, but then he'll be standing next to me doing squats in his underwear, making me rethink everything I thought I knew to be true. He's cool when he dances, because he's a fantastic dancer, but he also uses phrases like "Far out!" in all seriousness. Sometimes it seems as if he's trapped in the late seventies, early eighties, listening to disco and Cat Stevens and trying to convince us that we should all sit down and watch *MacGyver* reruns.[72]

I've made my peace with a lack of cool, because I've got awkward down pat. And you know how they have those sayings, like:

- "Fifty is the new thirty." (Said by fifty-year-olds who wish they were still thirty-year-olds).
- "Seventy is the new fifty." (Said by seventy-year-olds who wish they were still fifty-year-olds).
- "Sweatpants and a flannel shirt are the new little black dress." (That one's all me).

Well, I happen to have it on good authority[73] that awkward is the new cool.

ö Ö ö

---

[72] *Totally uncool. I'll take* Magnum, P.I. *any day.*

[73] *It's me. The good authority is me.*

Thank you for reading this book.

I have a free gift for you at
www.AmandaTurner.com/thankyou

*Do not expect to receive live animals or
an egg salad sandwich.*

Made in the USA
Columbia, SC
09 December 2022

73273310R00137